What People Are Saying About

Entwined Histories

All too few people write and comment on the rich connections between Britain and Poland, but Piotr Wilczek's collection of sparkling essays is an exceptional contribution. The broad range of topics, the variety of personalities introduced, and the high quality of the writing make for a truly exciting read.

Norman Davies, eminent historian of Europe and author of *Europe: A History* and *God's Playground: A History of Poland*

We are not usually the best judge of ourselves; others see us more clearly. In this book, a representative of one of Britain's closest European allies observes her with a sensitive eye, which is at once deeply appreciative but not yet dulled by over-familiarity. Piotr Wilczek's thinking about Britain and Poland together casts fresh and perceptive light on both.

Nigel Biggar (Lord Biggar of Castle Douglas, CBE), Regius Professor Emeritus of Moral Theology, University of Oxford, and author of *Colonialism: A Moral Reckoning*

These sparkling essays companionably guide us through courts, squares, clubs, bookshops, libraries, and restaurants. The appreciative perspective of a diplomat and scholar on centuries of British-Polish political and cultural interactions is enriching and often unexpected.

Richard Butterwick-Pawlikowski, Professor of Polish-Lithuanian History at University College London (SSEES), author of *The Polish-Lithuanian Commonwealth, 1733–1795: Light and Flame*

Wilczek is a rare breed of modern scholar-diplomat, and in these essays he casts a thoughtful gaze over a millennium of Polish history and five centuries of Anglo-Polish relations—, from Ioannes Dantiscus's introduction to the glittering court of Henry VIII to presenting his own credentials to Queen Elizabeth II by video link. Sharply observant, occasionally wistful, and always well-informed, Wilczek brings an intelligent sensitivity to the nuances of tradition, language, and customs in the historical dynamic between Poland and Britain. In the process, he opens up unexpected perspectives on Shakespeare, Byron, Conrad, and whether Polish Nobel Prize winners were really Polish.

Sir Gabriele Finaldi, Director of the National Gallery, London

Entwined Histories is a witty and often humorous collection of stylishly composed, personal, and scholarly essays, full of insights into the Anglo-Polish relationship of nations and their peoples. Like the best of the best of short films, Ambassador Wilczek's essays are both memorable and mercifully short.

Peter Fudakowski, screenwriter, producer, and director; creative producer of the Oscar-winning movie *Tsotsi*

From Pablo Neruda to Octavio Paz and Washington Irving, the list of ambassadors who write well is short. Piotr Wilczek— Poland's former ambassador to Washington, now in London—is an impressive addition to the list. Whether dealing with hefty matters of diplomacy or searching for the best Polish restaurants in London, Wilczek writes with wit, ease, and invention. And, like Joseph Conrad before him, he favours a subtle and nuanced English that most natives would envy.

Waldemar Januszczak, acclaimed art critic, documentary filmmaker, and long-standing columnist for *The Sunday Times*

These elegant and thoughtful essays, written in London, "a crossroads where history and the future intersect", treat many aspects of the cultural and political relations between Poland and the English-speaking countries where Piotr Wilczek has served as ambassador. The range is breath-taking: from historical notions of Poland as pivot of East and West, to Poland as a state of mind, to the "Golden Liberty" of the Polish eighteenth century. Those individuals who have connected Poland and Britain are considered: Byron; the wartime heroine Krystyna Skarbek; the novelist Joseph Conrad, "whose virtuosity was English; his moral imagination Central European"; and finally, the Ambassador himself, writing tenderly about London's bookshops, concert halls, restaurants, and haunts of exiles—, in his own wonderful phrase, "forever present, yet never fully at home".
Paulina Kewes, Helen Morag Fellow and Tutor in English Literature at Jesus College and Professor of English Literature at the University of Oxford

Piotr Wilczek's book of essays entitled *Entwined Histories* derives its unquestionable value from its elegantly balanced combination of literary, political, cultural, diplomatic-historical, and religious-studies analyses with observations based on the unique experiences of a top Polish diplomat in his eight years of service in Washington and London. *Cultural Memory*—, presented not with heavy theoretical elaboration, but rather erudite and unpretentious argumentation—, is an apt summary and common denominator of these nearly forty brief essays. Starting with the introduction on the essence of diplomacy entitled "On Quiet Exchanges", Wilczek presents a series of vignettes which succinctly and "quietly" get to their core point, each of which is fascinating, inspiring, and well-informed.
Holt Meyer, Professor of Slavic Literatures, University of Erfurt

A fascinating pot pourri of essays — on faith, history, culture, and life — which elegantly showcases the warmth, wit, and erudition of their author — Piotr Wilczek, the Polish Ambassador to the Court of St James's. His words — written with considerable élan — show that the Ambassador's role is not just to represent the interests of the home country abroad, but also to act as an interlocutor, helping both host and guest to a better understanding of one another and of the bonds that bind them.

Roger Moorhouse, historian of modern German and Polish history; author of *First to Fight: The Polish War 1939*

Soft-shoe is the art of sliding and sidestepping, while diplomacy is a dance of soft skills—communicating mutual needs with discretion. In his enlightening book of essays *Entwined Histories*, Poland's Ambassador to the United Kingdom, Piotr Wilczek, takes us behind closed doors as he moves through the salons of Washington, London, and Warsaw, building trust and fostering cooperation. From Donald Trump to Queen Elizabeth II and the enduring legacy of Winston Churchill, Wilczek leads the reader on a journey shaped by repeated acts of diplomacy, each grounded in a profound sense of historical awareness. Here is a diplomat who understands the quiet courtesy essential to relations between emissaries and a historian who thoughtfully explores how these bonds might be strengthened—for your freedom and ours, as Poles like to say.

Alex Storozynski, Pulitzer Prize-winning journalist, Chairman of the Kosciuszko Foundation, author of *The Peasant Prince: Thaddeus Kosciuszko and the Age of Revolution*

Memoirs of diplomats usually deal with political successes or failures. Few record their encounters with culture or present one culture through the lens of another. Piotr Wilczek succeeds in showing us a kinder and gentler side of diplomacy. He takes us for a leisurely walk through cultural events and significant contacts, and leaves us with the proposition that diplomacy is still possible.

Ewa M. Thompson, Professor Emerita of Slavic Studies at Rice University, author of *Imperial Knowledge: Russian Literature and Colonialism*

Ambassador Wilczek is not only a diplomat — he is also an intellectual historian, and in this delightful book, he pulls together so many strands: diplomatic, artistic, literary, and royal. I learnt much of interest and feel that both Poland and Great Britain were lucky to have such an erudite envoy, strengthening the ties between our two countries on so many different levels.

Hugo Vickers, royal biographer, historian, and broadcaster; author of acclaimed biographies of Elizabeth, the Queen Mother, and the Duchess of Windsor

ENTWINED HISTORIES

Essays on Poland, Britain,
and Cultural Memory

Piotr Wilczek

ENTWINED HISTORIES

Essays on Poland, Britain, and Cultural Memory

Piotr Wilczek

London, UK
Washington, DC, USA

CollectiveInk

First published by Chronos Books, 2026
Chronos Books is an imprint of Collective Ink Ltd.,
Unit 11, Shepperton House, 89 Shepperton Road, London, N1 3DF
office@collectiveinkbooks.com
www.collectiveinkbooks.com
www.chronosbooks.com

For distributor details and how to order, please visit the 'Ordering' section on our website.

Text copyright: Piotr Wilczek 2025

Paperback ISBN: 978 1 917704 54 0
eBook ISBN: 978 1 917704 70 0
PCN: 2025937960

A CIP catalogue record for this book is available from the British Library.

Design: Lapiz Digital Services

Printed in the UK by CPI Antony Rowe
Printed in the USA by Offset Paperback Mfrs., Inc.

The manufacturer's authorised representative in the EU for product safety is:
eucomply OÜ - Pärnu mnt 139b-14, 11317 Tallinn, Estonia,
hello@ eucompliancepartner.com, www.eucompliancepartner.com

We operate a distinctive and ethical publishing philosophy in all areas of our business, from our global network of authors to production and worldwide distribution.

To Krzysztof
For the roads we've walked, the ideas we've wrestled with, and the quiet wisdom you offered when I needed it most. Your presence is felt throughout.

CONTENTS

Acknowledgements

Understanding a country is not a solitary pursuit. It is a long conversation — conducted across languages, through books, in the quiet of libraries, and often over strong tea or slightly weaker wine. This book, though written in the first person, is the product of many such conversations, and I owe thanks to those who helped shape my understanding of Britain over the years.

First, to my late parents, whose decision in the early 1970s to insist I learn English was both unfashionable and farsighted. At a time when Russian was the safer bet in Polish schools, they chose instead to provide me with excellent teachers and the quiet conviction that language opens more than just dictionaries — it opens worlds.

To the late Adam Czerniawski — translator, poet, and guide — whose companionship, from the late 1980s until his passing in 2024, offered me a lens through which Britain appeared not as a museum piece but as a living, eccentric, deeply civilised place. I still hear his voice in the margins of these essays.

To St Anne's College, Oxford, which welcomed me as a Visiting Scholar in the Michaelmas Term of 1988. It was there, among ivy and intellectuals, that I first encountered the peculiar blend of rigour and understatement that marks British academic life — and which, to this day, I find both baffling and admirable.

To colleagues at the Warburg Institute and the University of East Anglia, who hosted me in the 1990s and tolerated my digressions with more grace than I deserved. Their encouragement and occasional corrections were formative, not only to my scholarship but also to my sensibility.

To the many British and Polish-British friends — diplomats, scholars, journalists, neighbours — who sustained me during my tenure as Poland's Ambassador in London. You are too numerous to name, and naming some would be unjust to the rest. But your insights, your hospitality, and your willingness to engage in long discussions about short passages of text have left their mark. This book is, in part, the trace of those exchanges.

And to my colleagues at the Polish Embassy in London, whose professionalism, commitment, and good humour have made our work a shared pleasure. Your support across the varied tasks of diplomatic life is reflected in more of these pages than you might think.

To all of you: my sincere thanks. If these essays manage to capture even a fraction of the complexity, generosity, and quiet humour I have found in Britain, it is because you helped me see them.

Introduction

Diplomacy is often mistaken for a theatre of declarations: flags, handshakes, and elaborately phrased communiqués. In reality, it is a quieter art — more rehearsal than performance. It takes place in corridors, over conversations that never quite make the minutes, and in the long, slow work of listening. These essays were written in that spirit. Not as policy, nor as memoir, but as a record of observations made in the margins of official life.

They follow the path of a diplomat who, while tending to protocol, could not help noticing the details that didn't fit. The way humour deflects tension. The quiet authority of libraries. The persistence of memory in places that prefer not to talk about it. They are an attempt to understand a country not only through its institutions, but through its habits — its literature, its silences, its particular kind of weather.

To work abroad in the service of one's own country is to live in a kind of double exposure. One becomes attuned not only to the landscape outside the window, but also to the one carried inward: history, assumptions, the quiet tug of familiar cadences. This doubleness is not disorienting — it is clarifying. It reveals how nations see themselves, and each other, and what they choose to remember.

This book is not about strategy or ceremony. It is about the smaller, more durable forms of connection: shared references, unexpected sympathies, the cultural echoes that carry across borders. The focus is not on grand events but on the texture of everyday encounters — the kind that reveal more, in the end, than headlines ever do.

Throughout, there runs an interest in exile, in what it means to rebuild lives far from home, and in how identities persist through displacement. It is a theme with deep resonance, especially in a city shaped by generations of those who arrived uninvited but stayed unforgotten. These stories, like many in the book, are not offered as conclusions, but as invitations to think further.

What follows is not a final word on anything. These are essays in the truest sense — explorations, digressions, a form of diplomacy in prose. They were written in the belief that culture speaks where politics cannot, and that understanding often begins with attention to detail.

Grosvenor Square, Mayfair, London

8 May 2025

To complete this book on the eightieth anniversary of VE Day is more than a coincidence of calendars. It is a quiet homage to the generations whose lives were shaped by the war — and to those who, in exile or alliance, in London or Warsaw, sustained the cultural and moral bonds that these essays seek to honour. The peace achieved in 1945 was imperfect and partial, especially from a Polish perspective, but the memory of that day reminds us how history's entwinements persist — not only in the archives, but in the lives we continue to lead.

PART I

CROSSING BORDERS, EMBRACING TRADITIONS

Twice Before the Crown, Once by Executive Order: A Diplomatic Journey

Few moments in a diplomat's career carry as much solemnity, grandeur, and historical weight as the presentation of letters of credence to a head of state. It is an event steeped in ceremony and rich in symbolism — a moment when personal achievement intersects with the vast continuum of history. Occasionally, it is also accompanied by an element of delightful unpredictability. I count myself among the rare few who have had the privilege of presenting credentials to Her Majesty Queen Elizabeth II not once, but twice — an anomaly that remains a distinctive aspect of my diplomatic journey.

My first experience of this ritual took place in the Commonwealth of the Bahamas, where I had the honour of serving as Poland's Ambassador, in addition to my simultaneous posting in the United States. The occasion bore all the hallmarks of diplomatic tradition, yet its setting was far removed from the gilded halls of European monarchy. And yet, the ceremony was prepared with the utmost care, exuding the kind of formality one might expect at a royal court. The Governor-General, a most elegant and gracious lady, represented the Queen with impeccable dignity, her every gesture embodying both tradition and grandeur. The bright tropical sun may have replaced London's mist, but within the walls of Government House, every detail was polished to perfection. This was no mere formality — after all, the British monarch remains the head of state in the Bahamas. At the time, I could not have imagined that five years later, I would find myself in a similar situation — this time, standing within the very heart of British tradition.

London provided an altogether different stage. The journey to Buckingham Palace was meticulously choreographed, each element infused with the quiet dignity that defines British ceremonial life. The Queen's ceremonial carriage, the stately procession through the gates, and the hushed efficiency of palace attendants all contributed to the sense of stepping into a tableau where history was both present and alive. Yet, this occasion took place via video link. The Queen was at Windsor Castle, and I was in Buckingham Palace, connected through a screen rather than sharing the same physical space.

At first, the Queen looked surprised when I mentioned that I was presenting letters of credence addressed to her for the second time — an unusual circumstance in diplomatic tradition. This virtual audience had its advantages. Instead of focusing on intricate rituals and formalities, it allowed for greater emphasis on the substance of the discussion itself. The twenty minutes spent in dialogue provided a meaningful opportunity to reflect on Poland's historic ties with Britain, ongoing bilateral cooperation between our two countries, and the broader landscape of diplomatic relations. The significance of this meeting extended beyond protocol; it was an example of how tradition and modernity can coexist within diplomatic engagements.

This experience stood in stark contrast to my time as Poland's Ambassador to the United States, where the presentation of credentials followed a completely different trajectory. Arriving in Washington not long before the presidential inauguration in January 2017, I found myself in an extraordinary situation. There was little time for newly appointed ambassadors to present their credentials to President Barack Obama before his departure, yet only those who had done so would be allowed to attend the inauguration of President Donald Trump. Faced with this logistical challenge, the U.S. Department of State devised an unprecedented solution — one that, to my knowledge, had never occurred before and has not been repeated since.

Instead of the traditional in-person presentation, we were asked to send our letters of credence to the White House, where they were formally accepted by an executive order signed by President Obama. This unusual process enabled us to be recognised as fully accredited ambassadors in time for the inauguration. In total, sixteen ambassadors found themselves in this unique situation, forming an informal group bonded by this unprecedented diplomatic arrangement.

Several months later, we were invited to meet President Trump — not to present credentials, but to take part in a gathering that closely resembled the customary credential presentation ceremony. Held in the spring of 2017, the event was meticulously organised. Each ambassador had only a few minutes with the President, proceeding in a carefully choreographed line to shake hands, exchange brief remarks, and pose for an official photograph. It was an efficient yet impersonal process, in stark contrast to the British tradition, where the monarch meets each ambassador individually, allowing for a more substantive conversation.

This juxtaposition of experiences highlights the profound differences in how diplomacy is conducted on either side of the Atlantic. The British approach emphasises continuity, ceremony, and individual engagement, reinforcing the deep-rooted history of monarchical diplomacy. The American model, by contrast, reflects the fast-paced, pragmatic nature of the country's political culture, where efficiency often takes precedence over tradition.

Reflecting on these varied experiences, I was struck by how each system embodies the values and customs of its respective nation. In Britain, the encounter with the monarch carries a sense of historical continuity, a recognition of the long-standing diplomatic relationships that define international engagement. In the United States, the emphasis is on procedure and practicality, where even an event as symbolic as presenting credentials must accommodate the rapid transitions of political office.

There is an undeniable elegance to the British approach to diplomacy, one that blends continuity with adaptability. The monarchy, steeped in centuries of tradition, remains a steadfast pillar of international engagement, yet it is not immune to change. The very fact that such a meeting could take place via video link demonstrated the monarchy's ability to balance historical precedent with contemporary necessity. The Queen's composure, her effortless command of the moment, and her ability to convey warmth even through a screen exemplified the refined artistry of British diplomacy.

As I departed Buckingham Palace, I reflected on the singularity of my experience — this rare distinction of having performed the same rite in two corners of the Commonwealth under vastly different circumstances. It was a reminder that diplomacy is shaped not only by treaties and policies but also by the personal encounters that weave together the stories of nations. To have had the opportunity to present credentials to the same monarch twice — albeit once to the Governor-General and the second time via a video link, never having met her in person — was at once a diplomatic curiosity, a historical footnote, and, above all, an unforgettable privilege.

The world of diplomacy is often imagined as one of rigid formality and carefully measured words, but in reality, it is moments like these — unexpected, personal, subtly revealing — that make it a truly fascinating vocation. Whether in person or across a screen, the act of engagement remains the same: a meeting of minds, a recognition of shared history, and the quiet assurance that, despite the passage of time and the evolution of diplomatic conventions, the essence of dialogue endures.

London or Washington?
The Question Everyone Asks

There is one question I am asked more often than any other. It has come from fellow ambassadors, seasoned politicians, sharp journalists, and even, on one occasion, from Her Majesty the Queen herself. The moment they learn that I previously served as Poland's ambassador to the United States before taking up my post in London, they invariably lean in with curiosity and ask: "Which do you prefer, Washington or London?"

The truth is that this question defies an easy answer. How does one compare the historical depth of London with the grand political theatre of Washington? The literary cafés of Bloomsbury with the power-lunching corridors of K Street? The majestic Thames with the imposing Potomac? Each city has a unique rhythm, its own way of asserting itself as the centre of the universe. And while both serve as crucial nodes in the global diplomatic network, they do so in distinctly different ways, shaped by their histories, political cultures, and social dynamics.

A fellow ambassador, newly posted to London, once asked me the same question but added, "Be honest — where did you have more fun?" I laughed, sensing that he expected tales of diplomatic intrigue and elegant soirées. The reality, of course, is that an ambassador's "fun" is measured differently from that of an ordinary traveller. In Washington, I spent my time in the gravitational field of the White House, engaging in conversations where every phrase was weighed, every gesture scrutinised. It is a city where diplomacy often unfolds under the glare of the media, where even a casual remark can turn into a headline. In London, by contrast, discussions tend to be more discreet, the art of diplomacy refined over centuries. Here, the most consequential conversations often take place not in the grandeur of government buildings but in the understated elegance of a club in St James's or the labyrinthine corridors of Westminster. Fun, in both places, is found in the exchanges of ideas and the constant engagement with some of the world's most interesting minds.

A British journalist once put it bluntly: "Which place was tougher?" I must admit, Washington has an intensity that London — despite its own brand of high-stakes diplomacy — cannot quite match. The relentless 24-hour political cycle, the deep divides, and the sense that every conversation is a strategic calculation define Washington. Power there is direct, transactional, and often unforgiving. London, on the other hand, operates with a different tempo, one that values nuance and understatement. British diplomacy is a long game, played with patience, subtlety, and an appreciation for history. If Washington is about shaping the immediate present, London is about balancing the weight of the past with the demands of the future.

Of course, not everyone shares this perspective. One Foreign Office official grinned at me and said, "Let's be honest, moving from Washington to London — it's a demotion, isn't it?" I smiled politely, though I could not have disagreed more. London remains a true global capital, a hub of finance, culture, and international affairs. If Washington is the cockpit of the world's most powerful nation, London is the crossroads where history and the future constantly intersect. The idea of a "demotion" in diplomatic terms is laughable — unless, of course, one believes that power is measured solely in military might. But any seasoned diplomat knows that influence takes many forms. Washington wields power through its institutions, alliances, and military capabilities. London, meanwhile, exerts influence through its unparalleled networks, its historical ties to every corner of the globe, and its command of the English language as the lingua franca of diplomacy, business, and culture.

As an academic by background, I have found London's intellectual scene particularly rewarding. Washington is a city of think tanks, where policy ideas are debated with the urgency of a breaking news cycle. London, on the other hand, is home to centuries-old institutions where discussions on politics, literature, and philosophy unfold with a more measured cadence. The difference is subtle but significant: Washington is a city where decisions are made; London is a city where ideas percolate.

On a personal level, life in London offers pleasures that Washington, for all its charms, struggles to match. The theatre scene alone is a marvel — where else can one see a Shakespeare production one evening and a daring new political drama the next? The bookstores of Charing Cross Road, the charm of Hampstead Heath, the unexpected delight of discovering a centuries-old pub tucked away down an alley — these are treasures that even the grand avenues of Washington cannot rival.

That said, I must acknowledge Washington's culinary evolution. When I first arrived there, finding a good cup of coffee was an odyssey. By the time I left, Michelin stars were multiplying, and a new generation of chefs was turning the city into a genuinely exciting gastronomic destination. London, of course, has long embraced the best of global cuisine, and one can travel the world in a single evening simply by dining across its many boroughs.

Ultimately, the question of "London or Washington?" is a bit like asking a parent to choose a favourite child. Both cities have tested and rewarded me in equal measure. Washington offered proximity to power and a front-row seat to history in the making. London provides the depth of tradition, the fluidity of conversation, and an enduring sense of place. Each city embodies a different philosophy of diplomacy — one steeped in pragmatism and the politics of the moment, the other rooted in continuity and a broader, global perspective.

Perhaps the best answer I can offer is that, as Poland's ambassador, I have had the great fortune to call both home. And so, when I am next asked this question — at a diplomatic reception, at a Downing Street meeting, or perhaps over a quiet cup of tea — I will smile, pause for a moment, and offer the only truthful answer: "It depends on the day."

London, the Other Polish Capital

The title of a 2014 exhibition at the Polish History Museum — *London: The Capital of Poland* — seemed at first glance like a provocation. Or at least a stretch. And yet, on closer inspection, it was something more precise: a historical truth hiding behind a metaphor. No city outside Poland has shaped Polish political and intellectual life quite like London.

When I arrived in the British capital in 2022 to begin my posting as Poland's Ambassador, I expected the usual accoutrements of diplomatic life — Whitehall's quiet grandeur, the hum of formality, the famously understated charm of British civility. What I did not expect was the subtle but persistent sensation that, in a way I could not quite explain, I had not entirely left Poland behind.

London has long played host to Polish exiles and institutions — not as a mirror of Warsaw, with its ministerial corridors and daily parliamentary furies, but as something more atmospheric: a capital of the Polish imagination. It was the Warsaw of exile, of memory and manuscript, of stubborn hope and worn trench coats, of émigré presses and Saturday school dictionaries. For decades, it was where Poland went when it had nowhere else to go.

The city wears this legacy lightly, as the English tend to do. But scratch the surface, and the traces are everywhere. In Kensington — elegant, reticent, and just eccentric enough — Polish bookshops once flourished, literary cafés buzzed with exiled argument, and entire neighbourhoods hummed in a tongue Churchill once called "unpronounceable, but indispensable". These were not just émigrés — they were a displaced intelligentsia, convinced that a country could be rebuilt in footnotes, editorials, and tea-stained manuscripts.

My first weeks in London took me to the Polish Institute and Sikorski Museum, named after General Władysław Sikorski, the leader of the wartime Polish government-in-exile. Entering its rooms is like stepping into a state that no longer exists — except, in some ways, it still does. Uniforms in glass cases, letters from battlefield command posts, photographs of men who fought for a homeland they could not return to: this is history, yes, but not just commemorative. It was, and remains, defiantly alive.

Britain became host to several exiled governments during the Second World War — French, Norwegian, Dutch — but the Polish exile was different in its duration. When the war ended, theirs did not. With Stalin's regime entrenched in Warsaw, the government-in-exile refused to disband. For decades, it operated from London, complete with ministries, ambassadors, and memoranda, insisting — rightly, as it turned out — that a Soviet satellite was no legitimate heir to the Polish Republic. Only in 1990 did it formally hand over its insignia to Lech Wałęsa, with the faintly triumphant air of a government proving history wrong.

But exile is not only about politics. It is also about life. Polish London was a city within a city: of theatres and newsrooms, of cafés and parishes, of passions imported from Lwów and Wilno, then rerouted through Hammersmith. *Wiadomości*, the émigré literary weekly, ran for decades, offering its readers not just reviews and essays but something harder to define: continuity.

No figure captured this world better than Mieczysław Grydzewski, editor of *Wiadomości*, keeper of flame and gossip, correspondent of scattered poets. His desk — still preserved — was a monument to organised chaos: manuscripts, letters, cigarette ash, and exasperated marginalia. Through his paper, he connected exiled writers with each other and with Poland, sustaining a literary culture that the Communist regime was trying very hard to silence.

There was also Jan Chodakowski, founder of the *Polonia* publishing house, who smuggled literature back across the Iron Curtain — books that couldn't be printed in Warsaw but could still be read in Wrocław. His *Puls Quarterly* kept the pulse of Polish intellectual life beating, even in exile. And of course General Anders, commander at Monte Cassino, who led not just troops but a diaspora. He and his soldiers made their homes here too — men who had marched from Siberia to Rome, only to find themselves, finally, on the District Line.

Today, their legacy persists. The Polish Social and Cultural Association (POSK) in Hammersmith still hosts plays, concerts, lectures — sometimes fiery, often poetic, always Polish. The Sikorski Museum remains a sanctuary of memory. The Saturday schools — some 130 of them across the UK, supported by the Polish Educational Society — continue to teach the language and history that the wartime exiles once feared might be lost.

The Polish Catholic Mission in England and Wales, founded in 1894, has long served as a spiritual and cultural anchor for Poles across the country — not only in London, but in cities and towns from Manchester to Southampton. Beyond its religious function, it has played a crucial role in sustaining language, tradition, and a sense of belonging. The churches in Ealing and Balham remain particularly vibrant, but they are part of a broader network of parishes where Polish heritage continues to be celebrated with both solemnity and joy.

Census data now tells us that Polish is the second most spoken language in the United Kingdom. What began as wartime refuge, then became intellectual resistance, has settled into something more permanent: community.

Of course, some of the old landmarks have faded. The bookshops are fewer, the journals have ceased publication. But the spirit remains. In the cafés of west London, one still hears arguments about history — delivered with that uniquely Polish mixture of erudition and vehemence. In the kitchens of Polish restaurants, cabbage still simmers in memory. In university lecture halls and newspaper columns, the voice of Polish London continues, if more quietly.

So no, London is not *the* capital of Poland. But it has long been *a* capital of Poland — a city of exile, of memory, of persistence. A place where a nation without a country once managed, with remarkable stubbornness, to carry on.

Czesław Miłosz once suggested that Poland is a state of mind as much as a geographical fact. If that's true, then London — rainy, stubborn, hospitable, and half in love with the past — remains one of its more vivid provinces.

Grosvenor Square: Where Histories Meet

London's Grosvenor Square stands as one of the city's most storied locations, a place where British aristocracy and transatlantic diplomacy have converged for centuries. Established in the early eighteenth century as the centrepiece of the vast Grosvenor Estate, the square has retained its air of exclusivity while adapting to shifting political, social, and architectural currents. Few places in London so seamlessly blend past and present, tradition and reinvention. Grosvenor Square has long been recognised as "one of the most aristocratic and fashionable places of residence in London" (*London Past and Present*, 1891).

When I moved from Washington, D.C. to London to take up my role as Poland's Ambassador to the United Kingdom, I anticipated many differences — architectural, cultural, and diplomatic. Yet, I did not expect that my residence in Grosvenor Square would provide such an uncanny bridge between my two worlds. From my reception room, I look out onto the former U.S. Embassy, its modernist façade designed by Eero Saarinen, once a bustling centre of American diplomacy in Britain. Though the embassy relocated to Nine Elms in 2017, its former site remains an icon of Grosvenor Square's American legacy, now being repurposed as a luxury hotel. The square's long history of transatlantic connections has created a setting where past and present constantly intertwine.

The sense of continuity is striking. There are moments when, strolling through the square, I experience a peculiar déjà vu — as if I am still in Washington, surrounded by the same symbols of American influence. Yet, reality soon asserts itself: the red buses, the faint chimes of Big Ben in the distance, the unmistakable rhythms of London life. My address, as one dinner guest wryly remarked, makes me "the most conveniently placed European for transatlantic diplomacy".

Grosvenor Square was laid out between 1725 and 1731 as part of the Grosvenor family's ambitious vision for Mayfair, an area that would soon become synonymous with wealth and influence. Designed on a grand scale, it was second only to Lincoln's Inn Fields in size and quickly attracted the upper echelons of society. The houses — large, imposing, and expensively finished — were built by an array of speculative developers, many of whom soon found themselves bankrupt. By 1738, nearly half had gone insolvent, though whether due to the financial pressures of the square's development or other misfortunes remains uncertain.

From its earliest days, Grosvenor Square became home to figures of title and consequence. Among them was the Duchess of Kendal, the long-time mistress of King George I, who resided here until her death in 1743. The Earl of Chesterfield, famed for his polished wit and scathing letters, lived in the square from 1733 to 1750. Lord North, the Prime Minister who presided over Britain's loss of the American colonies, also had his residence here, as did Henry Thrale, the wealthy brewer and patron of Samuel Johnson. The great lexicographer himself was a frequent visitor, as was Bishop Warburton, who in 1757 exchanged Bedford Row for the grandeur of Mayfair. The Marquess of Rockingham, Prime Minister from 1750 to 1782; Charles Townshend, Chancellor of the Exchequer during the turbulent years leading to the American Revolution; and Henry Addington, Prime Minister from 1792 to 1795, were also among its distinguished inhabitants. The 3rd Duke of Grafton, another former Prime Minister, called Grosvenor Square home, further cementing its reputation as a bastion of political and aristocratic power.

Despite its deep British aristocratic pedigree, Grosvenor Square has also played a pivotal role in transatlantic history.

This legacy began in 1785 when John Adams, the first U.S. Minister to Britain and later the second President of the United States, made No. 9 his home. His residence marked the beginning of an enduring Anglo-American presence that reached its zenith during the Second World War. The square became a hub of American diplomatic and military operations, with General Dwight D. Eisenhower's Supreme Headquarters located here. Such was the scale of the American presence that the square was informally dubbed "Eisenhower Platz" and "Little America".

The legacy of this period remains visible today in the form of statues and memorials honouring American leaders. President Franklin D. Roosevelt's statue, sculpted by Sir William Reid Dick, remains an enduring symbol of wartime alliance, while Robert Lee Dean's statue of Eisenhower commemorates the general's leadership. The Eagle Squadron Memorial pays tribute to the American pilots who joined the Royal Air Force before the United States formally entered the war. In 2011, a statue of President Ronald Reagan was unveiled in Grosvenor Square, honouring his role in ending the Cold War. It was taken down in 2021 during redevelopment work, but returned in February 2025 and now stands once again, side by side with the statue of General Eisenhower, in front of the former U.S. Embassy— soon to reopen as a luxury hotel. Its reappearance restores not just a familiar landmark, but an important piece of the square's layered transatlantic history.

What makes the Reagan statue especially striking—perhaps even unique in London—is its distinctly Polish element. At its base are plaques inscribed with words not only from Mikhail Gorbachev and Václav Havel, but also from Pope John Paul II and Lech Wałęsa. It may well be the only monument in the city where two Poles—one the spiritual leader of millions, the other a Nobel Peace Prize winner and former president—stand as voices alongside Reagan in marking the close of the Cold War.

Wałęsa's words read: "With the lever of American patriotism, he lifted up the world. And so today, in Prague, in Budapest, in Warsaw and Sofia, in Bucharest, in Kiev and in Moscow itself, the world celebrates the life of the great liberator." And John Paul II adds his own tribute, recalling Reagan's "abiding faith in the human and spiritual values which ensure a future of solidarity, justice and peace in our world".

The square has witnessed moments of upheaval as well. In 1777, the Neapolitan Ambassador was attacked here, while in 1727, an equestrian statue of King George I was defaced, revealing that even in its most refined spaces, London has always contained an undercurrent of disorder. More recently, in the wake of 9/11 and subsequent terrorist threats, security measures were significantly heightened around the U.S. Embassy, altering the square's once open and leisurely atmosphere.

Living in Grosvenor Square offers a constant interplay between past and present. One can hardly step outside without encountering a fragment of history — whether in the form of a weathered plaque, a dignified statue, or the remnants of a grand façade. Even the conversations of American tourists, debating whether the U.S. Embassy still operates from its former site, add to the square's distinctive charm.

Grosvenor Square, with its aristocratic grandeur and diplomatic significance, remains a testament to the lasting relationship between Britain and the United States. It has evolved from a noble enclave of London's elite to a symbol of transatlantic cooperation. And as I look out onto its storied façades, I am reminded that places, much like history, are never static — they are shaped, transformed, and redefined by those who pass through them.

PART II

SHARED HISTORIES, PARALLEL DESTINIES

Winston Churchill: A Dual Legacy in Britain and Poland

During my tenure as Poland's ambassador in Washington, I would often pass the British residence, where a statue of Winston Churchill stands resolutely, hand mid-gesture, as though still addressing the world. His image commands similar prominence within American institutions. On my first visit to the U.S. Embassy in London, I noted a large portrait of Churchill displayed behind the ambassador's desk — then occupied by my old acquaintance from Washington, Chargé d'Affaires Philip Reeker.

Such iconography would be difficult to imagine in the Polish Embassy. Not because Churchill is not respected — he is — but because in Poland his legacy remains profoundly ambivalent.

In Britain, Churchill is revered as the man who held the line when Europe was engulfed by tyranny: the wartime Prime Minister whose rhetoric galvanised a nation and whose resolve helped secure ultimate victory. Monuments, commemorative plaques, and institutions bearing his name are commonplace. His reputation as a national saviour is firmly established — and largely unchallenged.

In Poland, by contrast, Churchill's memory is far more contested. While his role in the Allied war effort is acknowledged, it is overshadowed by the consequences of the Yalta Conference in 1945, where Churchill, alongside Roosevelt and Stalin, participated in decisions that redrew Poland's borders and effectively acquiesced to Soviet domination. Though the Second World War ended in Europe with the defeat of Nazi Germany, for Poland it marked the beginning of another form of subjugation — this time under a communist regime imposed with Moscow's backing.

The term "Western betrayal" — though jarring to British ears — captures a genuine sense of historical grievance in

Polish political memory. Poland had fought from the very first day of the war, invaded by both Nazi Germany and the Soviet Union in September 1939. Polish forces continued the struggle abroad: its pilots distinguished themselves in the Battle of Britain; its intelligence officers contributed significantly to the Allied cause; its soldiers served with distinction across multiple theatres of war. Yet in the end, it was not invited to the victory celebrations in 1946, and its sovereignty was compromised for nearly half a century.

At Yalta, Churchill found himself navigating a perilous diplomatic landscape. The Red Army already occupied much of Eastern Europe. Roosevelt, gravely unwell and increasingly deferential to Stalin, was more concerned with hastening Japan's defeat than preserving Eastern European independence. Churchill attempted to negotiate for Poland's autonomy, pressing for guarantees of free elections and attempting to secure some semblance of pluralism. But, by that stage, the balance of power had shifted irrevocably. The outcomes, whatever the intentions, were interpreted in Poland as acquiescence.

The promises made — particularly the commitment to democratic elections — were swiftly broken. The communist regime installed in Warsaw did not derive its legitimacy from the Polish people but from Soviet tanks. Political opposition was suppressed, civil society dismantled, and religious institutions harassed. The notion that this fate had been sealed, at least in part, by decisions taken at Yalta — with Churchill's participation — has never fully disappeared from Polish historical consciousness.

In the Anglophone world, Churchill's post-war legacy is framed by his prescient warnings about Soviet expansionism. His "Iron Curtain" speech at Fulton, Missouri in 1946 is now seen as the inaugural address of the Cold War. In Britain and the United States, Churchill is remembered not only for his wartime leadership but for his early recognition of the danger posed by the Soviet empire. In Poland, however, this eloquent clarity came too late.

This divergence in memory helps to explain why Churchill is lionised in the West but regarded with reserve in the East. In London and Washington, he is synonymous with victory, resilience, and the defence of liberty. In Warsaw, he is a more equivocal figure — a symbol not of victory but of compromise.

Such judgements, of course, benefit from hindsight. One must acknowledge the extraordinarily complex circumstances in which Churchill operated. Faced with the prospect of prolonging the war, losing Stalin's cooperation, or imperilling European reconstruction, he chose what he believed to be the least damaging course. Whether one regards this as pragmatic statecraft or moral failure depends largely on one's vantage point. But in Poland, the cost of those decisions was felt acutely, and over generations.

It would be mistaken, however, to reduce Churchill's Polish legacy to simple condemnation. He remains a figure of fascination and considerable stature. Poles recognise that he did not act out of malice but out of calculation, and they understand — better than most — the dilemmas of realpolitik. What persists is not hatred but an unresolved reckoning.

Historical memory is not a ledger to be balanced, but a prism through which nations perceive the past. In Britain, Churchill continues to embody national courage. In Poland, he represents a tragic irony: that a statesman who spoke so movingly of freedom was unable to secure it for one of his staunchest allies.

It is, perhaps, precisely because of his greatness that the disappointment felt in Poland remains so acute. Churchill did not merely make decisions; he shaped destinies. For that reason, his legacy is — and will remain — a subject of reflection, admiration, and, inevitably, debate.

A Royal Connection: The Duke of Kent and Poland's Unwritten History

During my tenure as Poland's ambassador to the Court of St James's, I have had the privilege of meeting His Royal Highness Prince Edward, Duke of Kent, on several occasions. Our conversations have touched on a variety of subjects, but it was his recollections of his father, Prince George, Duke of Kent, that lingered longest in my mind. It is one of those elegant curiosities of history that a line of British royalty once brushed very close to Poland's own fate — a moment of "what if" that continues to fascinate.

Prince George, born in 1902, was the fourth son of King George V and Queen Mary — an urbane figure with a naval career, an international outlook, and a reputation for charm. In 1934, he married Princess Marina of Greece and Denmark, herself a great-granddaughter of Tsar Alexander II, thereby reinforcing the dense web of continental royal bloodlines. Their three children — Prince Edward, Princess Alexandra, and Prince Michael — have each, in their own way, played thoughtful, if discreet, roles in the world of diplomacy and public service. I have had the pleasure of meeting Princess Alexandra and Prince Michael as well, and each encounter has served to underscore how enduring the threads of Anglo-Polish connection truly are.

The Duke of Kent's link to Poland is not one of conventional diplomatic record, but of historical imagination — a footnote that might have been a headline. As Europe slid towards war in the late 1930s, Poland, trapped between the ambitions of Hitler and Stalin, looked increasingly exposed. It was then that a remarkable idea emerged: the possible restoration of the Polish monarchy with a British prince — specifically, Prince George — invited to assume the throne.

The logic was strategic as well as symbolic. At a moment of existential peril, the installation of a British royal as King of Poland would have signalled a powerful alignment with the Western Allies, while offering a unifying figurehead to a nation already bracing for occupation. General Władysław Sikorski, later Prime Minister of the Polish government-in-exile, is believed to have supported the plan. Whether he viewed it as serious policy or imaginative diplomacy remains unclear, but the very notion speaks to the closeness of Anglo-Polish relations at that decisive hour.

Of course, history had other ideas. The war intervened; politics hardened; and Prince George tragically died in a plane crash in 1942. The idea of a British king in Warsaw was consigned to the realm of counterfactual speculation. Yet the question remains: had things unfolded differently, would Prince Edward, born in 1935, be King of Poland today? It is an implausible prospect, yes — but a revealing one, too. It reminds us how delicately the fates of nations can hang on individual lives, and how, even in the darkest of times, the imagination of statesmen can entertain bold visions.

Prince Edward, for his part, has spent a lifetime in quiet and consistent public service. President of the All England Lawn Tennis and Croquet Club, Special Representative for International Trade and Investment, and a familiar face at the great rituals of state — he has never sought the limelight but has always carried his role with dignity. His affinity for Poland is particularly striking. The Polish Hearth Club (Ognisko Polskie), which his parents helped inaugurate during the Second World War as a haven for Polish émigrés, remains a part of his regular rounds. His presence at commemorative events has been both sincere and steadfast.

One such moment stands out. In 2020, to mark the 80th anniversary of the Battle of Britain, Prince Edward opened an exhibition at the Polish Embassy in London. He spoke movingly of the Polish pilots whose skill and courage played a vital role in the RAF's wartime efforts. "Their courage, resilience, and determination are legendary," he said — words that carried more weight for being delivered without fanfare.

This sort of engagement — respectful, consistent, unassuming — is often underestimated in today's era of declarative diplomacy. But it matters. The history of Polish–British relations is not only forged in treaty rooms and war rooms; it is sustained in salons, museums, and quiet conversations. Prince Edward understands this better than most.

There is something especially poignant in the knowledge that his father might once have become king of a nation that no longer has a monarchy. And yet, the point is not what didn't happen, but what did. The Polish monarchy was not restored, but the Polish nation endured. And throughout the trials of war, exile, and communist occupation, its friendship with Britain — though tested — remained real.

Reflecting on my meetings with Prince Edward, and with Princess Alexandra and Prince Michael, I am reminded of how much diplomacy happens beneath the radar. Royal families, for all their ceremony, often operate in the realm of soft influence — the kind that requires neither headlines nor fanfare to leave a lasting impression. The story of Prince George and the Polish throne may be an unwritten chapter, but the friendship it symbolised was very real — and continues to resonate.

History, after all, is not just a matter of what was. It is also a meditation on what might have been — and what, through quiet effort and enduring affinity, still might be.

At the Desk of Count Edward Raczyński

Seated at the desk once occupied by Count Edward Raczyński — under the quiet gaze of his portrait — I am reminded daily of the solemn weight of history. The room is spare, but it breathes with memory. A brass lamp, a worn photograph, the subtle scent of paper and polish — each detail seems steeped in the atmosphere of decisions once made in moments of national peril. For it was from here that one of Poland's most distinguished statesmen helped to shape the country's fate in the most trying century of its modern existence.

Raczyński's life and career — diplomat, foreign minister, ultimately President-in-exile — read like a précis of twentieth-century Polish history. But he was never merely a participant. He was, in the best sense, an architect: of alliances, of resistance, and of memory. His name, while still held in high regard in Polish diplomatic circles, deserves to resonate more widely in the consciousness of our British interlocutors, not only as a figure of wartime resilience but as one of the most principled emissaries Poland ever sent to these shores.

Born in 1891 in Zakopane into the noble Raczyński family — a lineage long associated with public duty and cultural patronage — Edward Bernard Maria Raczyński came of age as Europe slid towards crisis. He was educated in Leipzig, Kraków, and later at the London School of Economics, where he absorbed the rigours of economic theory and the nuances of liberal constitutionalism. His cosmopolitan education was not ornamental; it was the making of a mind that would navigate the moral and diplomatic tempests of the age with rare composure.

In 1934, he was appointed Poland's ambassador to the Court of St James's. It was a timely posting. The Continent was again beginning to tilt towards catastrophe, and Raczyński found himself at the epicentre of European diplomacy. On 1 September

1939, following the German invasion of Poland, it was he who formally informed the British government, invoking the Anglo-Polish alliance. It fell to Raczyński to articulate, with clarity and gravity, not only the immediate crisis but the broader principle at stake: the defence of European sovereignty against brute expansionism.

When the Polish government was forced into exile — first in France and subsequently in London — Raczyński's influence only grew. With fluent English, deep familiarity with British political culture, and an uncommon steadiness under pressure, he became a vital figure in sustaining Poland's voice abroad. At a time when moral arguments risked being drowned in the din of realpolitik, Raczyński's quiet authority kept Poland's cause not merely alive, but persuasive.

His tenure as Foreign Minister in the government-in-exile (1941–43) was marked by one of the most morally urgent diplomatic interventions of the war. On 10 December 1942, Raczyński issued a detailed communiqué — now known as Raczyński's Note — alerting the Allies to the systematic extermination of Jews in German-occupied Poland. It was among the earliest, clearest articulations of the Holocaust from an official source. He pleaded for recognition, for response, for action. The world's reaction was tragically muted. But Raczyński's decision to speak plainly, to document and to warn, remains one of the most courageous moments in wartime diplomacy.

His role extended to the delicate negotiations with the Soviet Union, notably over the fate of thousands of Polish officers and prisoners following the Soviet invasion of eastern Poland in 1939. It was Raczyński who represented Polish interests in fraught exchanges with Anthony Eden and Soviet counterparts such as Molotov and Maisky. His conduct was characterised not by naïveté but by resolve: a commitment to principles without illusions.

After the war, with Poland consigned to the Soviet sphere, Raczyński refused to retreat into quiet retirement. His estates confiscated, his homeland sealed behind the Iron Curtain, he transformed his residence at 8 Lennox Gardens into a centre of Polish émigré life. For decades, it served as a salon of resistance: intellectual, cultural, and political. Here, he kept alive the idea of a free Poland — long before it became a plausible prospect.

In 1979, at the age of 88, he was elected President of Poland-in-exile. The role was largely symbolic, but Raczyński brought to it the weight of a life steeped in statesmanship. Blindness had by then overtaken his eyesight, but not his clarity of thought. He wrote, received visitors, encouraged young émigrés, and sustained — almost alone — the sense that Poland's constitutional continuity had not been severed, merely suspended. He served until 1986, handing over not merely an office but a moral legacy.

Now, decades later, I find myself in the very room from which Raczyński once wrote his dispatches, met his visitors, and pondered his country's fate. The desk remains much as it was — more than a relic, a reminder. For Raczyński, diplomacy was not performance. It was service. His tools were language, precision, and patience. He understood that diplomacy required moral clarity as much as strategic finesse, and that the long game was often the only one worth playing.

In an era of fast-turnover envoys and fleeting headlines, Raczyński's career offers a salutary contrast. He represented a style of diplomacy rooted in principle, culture, and continuity. His notion of patriotism was not narrow nationalism, but a deep fidelity to the civic and moral traditions of the Polish state. And his understanding of Britain — its temperament, its institutions, its strategic imagination — was profound.

It is difficult, from the vantage of the present, not to feel a certain reverence for his example. As Poland and Britain now confront new challenges — geopolitical, economic, and cultural — it is figures like Raczyński who remind us of what diplomacy can, at its best, embody. Not simply the negotiation of terms, but the defence of civilisation.

As I rise from his desk, glance again at the portrait — those eyes, composed but unyielding — I am reminded that the work of preserving liberty, sovereignty, and dignity is never done. Raczyński's legacy is not only to be remembered; it is to be upheld.

And so we continue, in his shadow, but also in his light.

A Portrait of Resolve: General Maczek and Poland's Exile in Britain

In my office at the Polish Embassy in London hangs a portrait of General Stanisław Maczek, his signature boldly inscribed beneath. This image serves not merely as decoration but as a daily reminder of the virtues he so fully embodied: integrity, resilience, and sacrifice. More profoundly, it symbolises Poland's significant contribution to the Allied victory in the Second World War, and the enduring bonds forged between Poland and Britain during one of history's most testing periods.

Born on 31 March 1892 in Szczerzec near Lwów (now Lviv, Ukraine), Stanisław Maczek entered a world in which the very notion of a Polish state remained a distant aspiration. He studied philosophy and Polish philology at the University of Lwów, yet his aspirations extended beyond the academic. During his student years, Maczek joined the Riflemen's Association, a patriotic paramilitary organisation that helped prepare a generation of young Poles for the struggle to reclaim their nation's independence.

The outbreak of the First World War saw him conscripted into the Austro-Hungarian Army. Serving with distinction on the Italian front, Maczek demonstrated not only personal bravery but also a remarkable flair for tactics. When Poland regained its independence in 1918, he joined the reborn Polish Army and quickly advanced through its ranks. His leadership during the defence of Lwów in the Polish–Ukrainian War, and later during the Polish–Soviet War, earned him a reputation for initiative, skill, and moral authority.

By September 1939, on the eve of the Second World War, Maczek was in command of the elite 10th Motorised Cavalry Brigade — Poland's only fully motorised unit at the time. Faced with invasion from Nazi Germany in the west and the Soviet

Union in the east, he led his brigade in a series of fighting withdrawals. Though forced into retreat by overwhelming enemy pressure, he managed to preserve the cohesion and morale of his troops under harrowing conditions. His decision to lead his men across the border into Hungary ensured their survival and allowed many of them to continue the fight alongside the Allies in the years to come.

After the fall of France in 1940 — where he and his fellow Polish soldiers had once more fought against German forces — Maczek made his way to Great Britain. It was in Scotland that his leadership took on renewed significance, as he painstakingly assembled the 1st Polish Armoured Division from among his exiled compatriots. Training was rigorous, but Maczek instilled in his men not only discipline and tactical proficiency, but also a deep sense of purpose.

When the division landed in Normandy in August 1944, they quickly demonstrated their worth. Their most decisive engagement came during the Battle of the Falaise Pocket. Under Maczek's astute command, Polish troops played a crucial role in closing the Falaise Gap, thereby encircling a large portion of the retreating German army. This action dealt a serious blow to the enemy's strength in the West and hastened the Allied advance. Even amid the brutal realities of war, Maczek remained acutely mindful of civilian lives. When liberating towns in Belgium and the Netherlands — notably Breda — he ordered operations to be conducted with exceptional care, avoiding unnecessary damage or casualties. The people of Breda, deeply grateful, granted him honorary citizenship, a gesture that reflected their lasting esteem.

Yet for General Maczek, the Allied victory in 1945 brought with it personal sorrow. With Poland falling under Soviet control, he was left in exile. The communist authorities stripped him of his citizenship, and although he had fought under British command, he never formally served in the

British Armed Forces — thus he was denied a military pension. Settling in Edinburgh, the highly decorated general took modest employment as a barman at the Learmonth Hotel. It was a role far removed from his wartime achievements, yet one which he carried out with quiet dignity. Most patrons remained unaware that the courteous bartender behind the counter was a former battlefield commander whose name was revered across liberated Europe.

Despite adversity, Maczek retained his dignity and sense of purpose. His small flat in Edinburgh became a discreet gathering place for fellow Polish exiles and former soldiers, who continued to refer to him respectfully as "General". These informal reunions offered solace and solidarity to a displaced community bound by shared sacrifice and enduring loyalty.

Recognition of Maczek's contribution came belatedly. Upon learning of his circumstances, the Dutch government discreetly arranged a pension, enabling him to live out his final years with dignity. This gesture symbolised the profound respect the Dutch people held for the man who had liberated their towns with such humanity and care.

It was only with the political transformations of the late twentieth century that justice began to catch up with history. In 1989, following the collapse of communism, the Polish government issued a formal apology for the injustices he had suffered. In 1994, in a moment of symbolic and heartfelt restitution, President Lech Wałęsa travelled to Edinburgh to confer upon the 102-year-old general Poland's highest honour — the Order of the White Eagle.

General Maczek died on 11 December 1994. In accordance with his wishes, he was laid to rest in the Polish military cemetery in Breda, among the soldiers of his division. The ceremony was attended by dignitaries from Poland, the Netherlands, and the United Kingdom, honouring a commander whose legacy had finally received the recognition it so richly deserved.

The recent publication of *The Price of Victory*, Maczek's memoirs (2024), brings his story to a new generation of English-speaking readers. Jennifer Grant's careful editorial work not only highlights the military strategies and battlefield experiences, but also the ethical compass and personal sacrifice that defined Maczek's life and leadership.

General Maczek's story resonates far beyond military history. It speaks to themes of exile, moral courage, and the long shadow of unacknowledged service. His life serves as a powerful reminder that true honour lies not only in public acclaim but in steadfast fidelity to principle, even when history forgets or overlooks it.

Today, as I glance at his portrait hanging in my office, General Maczek's steady gaze seems to offer both a lesson and a challenge — to remember, and to live by, the enduring virtues of honour, compassion, and courage that he exemplified. In commemorating Maczek, we honour not just a brilliant soldier, but the unbroken spirit of a nation that carried its ideals through exile and adversity, refusing ever to surrender them.

The Legacy of Krystyna Skarbek:
Courage Beyond Borders

Wandering along the serene streets of Kensington recently, I paused before the unassuming façade of 1 Lexham Gardens. A blue plaque, quietly dignified, announces that Krystyna Skarbek — known in Britain as Christine Granville — lived here between 1949 and 1952. Such simplicity belies the extraordinary story of the woman who once inhabited these rooms. Skarbek's life, punctuated by courage, espionage, and tragedy, stands as a compelling testament to the resilience and complexity of a Polish heroine, whose exploits continue to captivate and inspire.

Born in Warsaw on 1 May 1908, Krystyna was a child of privilege and paradox. Her father, Count Jerzy Skarbek, epitomised the declining Polish aristocracy, a man fond of horses, hunting, and extravagant living. Her mother, Stefania Goldfeder, brought the wealth of Warsaw's Jewish merchant class. Her father, sensing an early spark of adventure in his daughter, christened her affectionately "Vesperale", after the evening star that appeared at her birth — a symbol, perhaps, of the dazzling yet transient brilliance her life would embody.

The outbreak of the Second World War ignited Skarbek's restless spirit. She swiftly volunteered her services to Britain's Special Operations Executive (SOE), becoming one of its earliest female recruits. Skarbek's skills — her fluency in multiple languages, her athletic prowess, and her fearless disposition — rendered her invaluable. She was dispatched across treacherous terrains, tasked with smuggling intelligence and coordinating resistance networks deep behind enemy lines.

One of her earliest missions required skiing perilously across the Carpathian Mountains into occupied Poland, delivering vital intelligence and morale-boosting propaganda. Her physical courage and intuitive grasp of espionage quickly became legendary. Her superior officer at SOE admiringly described her as "the bravest person I have ever known, the only woman who longed for danger. With dynamite, she could accomplish anything but consume it."

In 1941, Skarbek found herself arrested by the Gestapo in Budapest, alongside fellow agent and lover Andrzej Kowerski. Facing imminent execution, her resourcefulness never wavered. Biting her tongue until blood filled her mouth, she feigned advanced tuberculosis so convincingly that her captors, repulsed and terrified of infection, released them both. It was precisely this audacious ingenuity that earned Winston Churchill's admiration, reputedly declaring her "my favourite spy".

Yet it was her audacity in the Vercors region of France in 1944 that cemented her legend. Parachuted into southern France, Skarbek took on the alias Pauline Armand, serving as a liaison officer to Francis Cammaerts, a pivotal figure in the French Resistance. When Cammaerts and two other agents were seized by the Gestapo, she embarked on a rescue mission of remarkable daring. Marching brazenly into enemy headquarters, she announced herself as a British intelligence officer and the niece of General Montgomery, offering a stark ultimatum: release the prisoners immediately, or face retribution from rapidly advancing Allied forces. Her bluff succeeded spectacularly; all three men were released unharmed.

Despite the accolades — including the George Medal, an OBE, and France's Croix de Guerre — the post-war years proved less kind. The very attributes that had made Skarbek an exemplary spy — courage, cunning, and adaptability — found no natural place in peacetime Britain. Her post-war life descended into obscurity and hardship, a poignant reflection on the ephemeral nature of heroism once the guns fall silent. She took humble employment as a stewardess aboard passenger liners, the medals that could have adorned a general discreetly tucked away.

Tragically, the peril Skarbek once courted with defiance claimed her in a senseless act of violence. On 15 June 1952, she was murdered by a former colleague obsessed by unrequited love. During that same walk through Kensington, guided by a friend, I entered what is now the 1 Lexham Gardens Hotel — then known as the Shelbourne Hotel — and was shown the very spot in the lobby where she collapsed after being fatally stabbed. Her death, after surviving the Gestapo and countless missions behind enemy lines, remains a cruelly ironic epilogue to her remarkable life.

Standing before the blue plaque at Lexham Gardens, I felt the quiet Kensington street recede, replaced momentarily by the tempestuous scenes of Skarbek's existence — Carpathian snows, French forests, and the desperate intrigues of war. Her story encapsulates the essence of courage: not merely facing danger, but actively seeking it, defying convention, and breaking barriers. Her life illustrates vividly how history's true complexities often reside not in grand gestures alone, but in quiet resilience and unyielding spirit.

Krystyna Skarbek's legacy speaks powerfully to the nuanced intersections of identity, bravery, and tragedy. Her actions during the war challenged perceptions of gender and national identity, demonstrating how a Polish-Jewish woman could decisively shape the course of events amidst Europe's darkest hour. Her remarkable narrative serves as a poignant reminder of the unseen and often uncelebrated sacrifices that underpin history.

In the Shadow of Memory:
Revisiting the Polish-Jewish Past

The shared history of Poles and Jews is one of profound complexity, spanning over a thousand years of coexistence, cultural exchange, and, at times, painful division. Few relationships between nations and communities have been so deeply interwoven, shaping not only the landscape of Polish history but also the broader currents of European and Jewish civilisation. The Jewish presence in Poland, which began as early as the medieval period, developed into a vibrant cultural and intellectual centre, one that profoundly influenced the religious, economic, and artistic life of the region. For centuries, Poland was home to the largest Jewish population in the world, a fact that underscores its significance as a site of both Jewish creativity and tragic destruction.

It is not possible to engage with Polish-Jewish history without acknowledging the fundamental duality of its nature. On one hand, Poland offered a refuge to Jews who faced persecution elsewhere in Europe, allowing them to cultivate rich traditions and intellectual life. The Talmudic scholarship of Polish Jewry was among the most sophisticated in the world, and cities such as Kraków, Lublin, and Wilno became centres of Jewish learning. The rise of Hasidism in the eighteenth century, originating in Polish and Ukrainian lands, marked another transformative moment in Jewish spiritual life, shaping religious traditions far beyond Poland's borders. Moreover, the emergence of Yiddish literature and theatre in Poland contributed to a flourishing Jewish cultural sphere, one that enriched not only Jewish communities but also Polish society at large.

Yet, alongside these moments of cultural efflorescence were episodes of profound hardship. The relationship between Poles and Jews was not without tension, and economic and social disparities often led to periods of conflict. The partitions of Poland at the end of the eighteenth century introduced new challenges for Jewish communities, as they were now subjected to the policies of foreign empires — Russia, Prussia, and Austria — each of which imposed differing degrees of assimilation and restriction. The nineteenth and early twentieth centuries saw the rise of new ideological currents — Zionism, socialism, and Polish nationalism — all of which intersected in complex ways with Jewish identity and Polish political aspirations. The multiculturalism of the Polish–Lithuanian Commonwealth, once a defining characteristic of the region, began to erode under the pressures of modern nationalism and the transformations of industrial society.

The twentieth century marked an irrevocable rupture in Polish-Jewish history. The Holocaust devastated the Jewish population of Poland, eradicating centuries of vibrant communal life. The destruction of Jewish communities, the loss of cultural and intellectual heritage, and the near-total annihilation of Poland's Jewish population during the Second World War constitute an unfathomable loss. The post-war years saw further dislocation, with many of the remaining Jewish survivors leaving Poland. This exodus was exacerbated in 1968 when the Communist authorities in Poland launched an antisemitic campaign, leading to the expulsion of thousands of Jews, many of whom had already lost much during the war. This state-sponsored persecution, disguised as an attack on alleged "Zionist elements", further fragmented what remained of Polish Jewry, deepening historical wounds that have taken decades to acknowledge and address.

Despite these historical wounds, recent decades have witnessed renewed efforts to engage with and commemorate Poland's Jewish past. Scholarly research, cultural initiatives, and museum projects have sought to recover the memory of Jewish life in Poland, moving beyond narratives of destruction to also celebrate the intellectual and artistic contributions of Polish Jewry. The *Polin: Studies in Polish Jewry* series, which has been instrumental in advancing academic research on Polish–Jewish relations, is one such example. The establishment of the POLIN Museum of the History of Polish Jews in Warsaw, which opened in 2013, represents another milestone in this process, providing an interactive and multifaceted account of the millennium-long Jewish presence in Polish lands.

Two significant experiences during my tenure as ambassador have particularly shaped my understanding of this shared history. The Hanukkah celebration held in Washington, D.C., in 2018, marking both Poland's centenary of independence and Israel's 70th anniversary, was a moment of profound historical resonance. The event, co-hosted by the Polish and Israeli embassies, was an acknowledgment of the deep historical ties between Poles and Jews. Israeli Ambassador Ron Dermer and I lit the Hanukkah menorah, symbolising resilience and continuity, while the accompanying discussions reflected on the evolving relationship between Poland and Jewish communities worldwide. Cultural performances, including Yiddish songs reinterpreted for contemporary audiences, served as reminders of the artistic legacy that Jewish communities cultivated on Polish soil. It was a moment that underscored the continuing importance of Jewish heritage in Polish history and the need to engage in ongoing dialogue.

Equally significant was the conference *Jews in Polish and German Lands: Encounters, Interactions, Inspirations*, held in London in 2025 to mark the launch of *Polin: Studies in Polish Jewry*, Volume 37. Hosting the concluding session of the conference at the Polish Embassy was a deeply meaningful occasion. The conference brought together scholars from multiple disciplines to explore the intricate web of connections between Jewish communities in Poland and Germany, moving beyond simplistic national frameworks to consider shared experiences and intellectual exchanges. Among the key figures present was Ambassador Tzipi Hotovely of Israel, whose remarks underscored the importance of engaging with history in a way that fosters mutual understanding rather than division. A particularly illuminating keynote lecture by Dr Anne Christin Klotz examined Jewish humour as both a form of resistance and an expression of communal solidarity in 1930s Poland, shedding light on the ways in which culture can serve as a means of navigating political adversity.

These events, taken together, suggest that the study of Polish–Jewish relations is not merely an academic exercise, but a crucial endeavour in shaping historical consciousness. The past cannot be changed, but the way it is remembered and interpreted has profound implications for the present. The re-engagement with Poland's Jewish heritage, whether through museum exhibitions, literary studies, or diplomatic dialogue, is part of a broader attempt to construct a more nuanced and informed historical narrative.

It is evident that no single narrative can fully encapsulate the depth of the Polish-Jewish experience. This history is too multifaceted, too rich in its complexities, to be reduced to a singular perspective. Yet, by continuing to explore and engage with it, by fostering dialogue rather than retreating into hardened positions, a greater understanding can emerge — one that recognises both the glories and the tragedies of the past. This, ultimately, is the task of history: to illuminate, to challenge, and to deepen our understanding of the world we inhabit.

As Poland continues to reflect on its Jewish past, it is imperative to do so not merely as a matter of national memory, but as an integral part of European and Jewish history. The study of Polish–Jewish relations is not an isolated field, but one that speaks to broader questions of identity, belonging, and historical responsibility. It reminds us that history is not static, but constantly reinterpreted, shaped by new research, new voices, and new perspectives. If there is one lesson to be drawn from this long and entangled past, it is that history should never be seen as a matter of division, but as a source of dialogue and deeper understanding.

The BBC Polish Section: A Line to London, a Lifeline to Truth

In Poland in the 1970s and '80s, the act of turning on a radio could feel like a small rebellion. Among the crackle of shortwave frequencies and the hiss of Soviet-era jamming devices, the BBC Polish Section cut through with something that felt both improbable and vital: calm, well-informed, unsentimental truth. It wasn't just news — it was a lifeline.

I was among the many who tuned in, discreetly and with due caution. For those of us living under censorship and ideological exhaustion, the BBC Polish Service was not simply broadcasting information; it was offering perspective. I remain grateful to those voices on the airwaves — Poles and Britons alike — who managed, with a mixture of cool professionalism and quiet daring, to report the world as it was, rather than as our government insisted it be.

The service had been born, in suitably dramatic fashion, on 7 September 1939 — barely a week after the German invasion and just days after Britain declared war. Its first broadcast featured Poland's Ambassador to London, Edward Raczyński, offering a defiant reminder that Poland, though invaded, had not surrendered. In a country where simply owning a radio was enough to invite arrest under the Nazis, these messages from the BBC were more than journalistic dispatches; they were acts of resistance.

During the occupation, Poles listened in secret. And then, under Communism, they continued to do so. The methods of repression changed, but the impulse to hear the truth — to know what was happening in the world, unfiltered by dogma — remained constant. The Polish Section survived jamming, propaganda, and periodic attacks from Party apparatchiks. Through it all, it kept talking.

It didn't only report politics. It taught English, discussed literature, and offered glimpses into a world we were forbidden to know. For a generation of Poles, it was an introduction to global civility. The tone was modest, measured, and mercifully free of ideology. In a world of slogans and suspicion, it was oddly reassuring to hear a weather report from London.

When Communism collapsed and Poland found itself, at last, free to face the future on its own terms, the BBC Polish Section adapted. In the 1990s, it began to cooperate with Polish public broadcasters, launching programmes like *Reflektor* and *Magazyn Europejski*, and embracing the possibilities of digital audio and online transmission. It even pioneered Poland's first mobile news service — an elegant irony, given how carefully we had once hidden our radios from view.

During the run-up to Poland's accession to the European Union, the BBC's Polish team offered explanations, context, and institutional clarity — something not always forthcoming from Brussels or Warsaw. It was, once again, an honest broker in a noisy, partisan world.

And then, in 2005, it ended. The BBC World Service, shifting its strategic priorities, closed the Polish Section in December of that year. No protests, no headlines — just a quiet farewell after 66 years of uninterrupted service. It was a logical decision in many ways: Poland was now a democracy, with a boisterous media of its own. But for many of us, the closure marked the end of something more intimate — a relationship that had helped carry us through a half-century of disinformation.

One cannot speak of the Polish Section without mentioning its people — particularly figures like Jan Nowak-Jeziorański, wartime courier, voice of the underground, and later the director of Radio Free Europe's Polish Service. These were not broadcasters in the conventional sense. They were, by necessity, historians, moralists, teachers, and occasionally smuggled truth-tellers. What they offered was more than information; it was trust.

Today, as censorship returns in various guises around the world — algorithmic, autocratic, or simply financial — the legacy of the BBC Polish Section seems less like a Cold War relic and more like a handbook. From Eritrea to Belarus, international broadcasters still carry out the same work: providing facts where only fiction is permitted. Radio Erena, broadcasting into Eritrea from Paris, faces signal jamming and state harassment, much as the BBC once did. Radio Free Europe continues to operate in parts of the former Soviet sphere, broadcasting to populations who know that local news is rarely what it claims to be.

The relationship between dictatorship and media is nothing if not consistent. Where power consolidates, truth is treated as subversion. In Nicaragua, journalists still file reports as if their lives depend on it — because, quite often, they do. Independent media in such places becomes not merely a profession but a form of civil resistance.

Even in regimes not actively hostile to media freedom, a little transparency can be a dangerous thing. Some authoritarian leaders allow just enough press scrutiny to monitor corruption or gauge public sentiment — tools of control, not emancipation. But even this grudging tolerance can backfire. Honest reporting has a tendency to spread.

The story of the BBC Polish Section is a reminder that information, when delivered clearly and calmly, has a way of getting through. It may take years. It may not change everything. But it reaches people. And once heard, the truth is difficult to unhear.

For those of us who once waited each evening to tune in, carefully adjusting the dial to catch a familiar London voice, that memory still lingers — not in nostalgia, but in gratitude. The signal may have faded. The message has not.

Poland and the Essence of the West: A Contemplative Perspective from the Centre of Europe

"Poland is not East or West. Poland is at the centre of European civilisation. It has contributed mightily to that civilisation. It is doing so today by being magnificently unreconciled to oppression."

So said Ronald Reagan, and it remains one of the more succinct articulations of Poland's singular place in the European story.

To understand the West through Polish eyes is to understand both kinship and distance. Poland belongs fully to the Western tradition, but not always comfortably. Its history, religious inheritance, and geopolitical position have placed it at once within and alongside the broader Western current. This is not a contradiction — it is a vantage point. And it has shaped Poland's relationship with the United Kingdom, from wartime alliance to present-day partnership, as well as its role as a bridge to Europe's Eastern frontier.

"The West" is not a matter of longitude. It is a civilisation — part inheritance, part aspiration — comprising a set of ideas: Christian ethics, Enlightenment reason, rule of law, constitutional order. Poland has absorbed these elements, refracted them through its own experience, and at times held fast to them when others did not.

The story begins with a baptism. In 966, Poland entered Latin Christendom, anchoring itself in the Western Church and, by extension, Western culture. This alignment — decided not by Rome but by a Slavic ruler, Mieszko I — was no minor affair. It placed Poland apart from its Orthodox neighbours and set it on a course that would endure despite invasions, partitions, and ideological experiments. If religion is the spine of Western identity, Poland has never doubted its own posture.

Centuries later, the Polish–Lithuanian Commonwealth offered one of the most curious and compelling experiments in Western pluralism. Catholics, Protestants, Jews, Orthodox Christians, and Muslims coexisted (mostly) in relative peace — an arrangement not matched elsewhere in Europe at the time. The Commonwealth's republican traditions, its *Golden Liberty* and elective monarchy, drew the admiration of Enlightenment thinkers abroad, including some in Britain. Of course, the system eventually failed — undermined from within and devoured from without — but its memory has lingered as a sign that liberty, for all its risks, had deep roots in the Polish political imagination.

The nineteenth century saw Poland vanish from the map — partitioned by its neighbours, denied a state, but never a nation. It was during this long century of nonexistence that the Catholic Church became not merely a religion but a vessel of memory and identity. Priests were teachers, churches became archives, and the Polish language was kept alive through prayer and poetry.

Britain, in those years, played host to Poland's exiled statesmen and thinkers. Adam Jerzy Czartoryski, though based in Paris, maintained diplomatic ties with London and sought British support for the Polish cause. Later, Józef Piłsudski's circle kept close watch on British foreign policy. Polish exile has long had a British dimension.

Then came the catastrophes of the twentieth century. Occupation, genocide, and totalitarianism. Yet through it all, Poland's Western orientation did not buckle. If anything, it hardened. The election of Karol Wojtyła as Pope John Paul II in 1978 was a cultural earthquake. Suddenly, the head of the Catholic Church was a Pole — and one who had lived under both Nazism and Communism. His voice lent moral force to the Solidarity movement and, in alliance with Reagan and Thatcher, helped tilt the Cold War towards its end. The Polish

49

question was no longer confined to history books; it was back on the geopolitical table.

Since then, Poland has re-entered Western institutions: NATO in 1999, the EU in 2004. But re-entry is not the same as assimilation. Poland's political and cultural instincts — rooted in Catholic moral philosophy, wary of technocratic overreach, resistant to radical social engineering — have not always aligned with the increasingly secular progressivism of Western Europe. This divergence is not ideological defiance but historical fidelity. The West, Poland insists, is not only the Enlightenment but also Jerusalem and Rome.

Security, meanwhile, has reinforced Western bonds. Poland is now one of NATO's most active and committed members. Its support for Ukraine has been resolute, its cooperation with Britain deep and ongoing. Few nations speak more fluently the language of deterrence. Unlike some of its partners, Poland needs no reminding of what happens when deterrence fails.

Culturally, Poland's Western identity is equally textured. Over a million Poles now live in Britain. They have brought with them not only work and energy, but a commitment to education, family, and faith. The Saturday schools, parish communities, and Polish-language newspapers scattered across the UK speak to a dual fidelity: to integration, yes, but not at the expense of memory.

The Polish Catholic Mission in England and Wales continues to serve both spiritual and cultural needs — reminding one that religion, far from receding, remains central to many Poles' understanding of what it means to be Western. Poland's religiosity is not an exotic holdover but a core identity marker. That may jar with certain European assumptions, but it also offers a useful corrective: that liberal democracy need not be post-Christian to function.

What Poland reveals is that "the West" is not a homogenous block but a mosaic of nations, some more ancient than others, each holding different emphases. For Poland, freedom is not the abstraction of Enlightenment salons, but something tested by tanks and secret police. For Poles, the past is not a museum but a rehearsal for the present.

This makes Poland an awkward partner at times — but an essential one. Its patriotism can seem old-fashioned, its sense of tragedy unfashionable. And yet, these are precisely the qualities that make it valuable. It remembers things others forget. It insists on history in an age that prefers amnesia.

And if this vision at times sits uneasily within the prevailing orthodoxies of Western Europe, that too is part of the dialogue.

So, what is the West, seen from Warsaw? It is a tradition to which Poland belongs by baptism, by blood, by conviction. It is Athens, Rome, and Jerusalem — but also Gniezno, Kraków, and the Gdańsk shipyard. It is the hope that freedom matters, that truth exists, and that culture is worth the fight.

And in that refusal to forget what others overlook lies a clarity the rest of Europe may yet come to admire.

Why a Republic Celebrates a Coronation

In early 2024, I found myself engaged in an intriguing conversation with a group of Poles and a distinguished British aristocrat. As we exchanged pleasantries, one of my compatriots mentioned that in 2025, Poland would celebrate the 1000th anniversary of the coronation of its first king, Bolesław Chrobry. The British interlocutor, with evident curiosity and a hint of scepticism, responded: "But Poland is a republic, isn't it?" This single question encapsulated much. Why would a republic commemorate a royal coronation? What significance does a medieval ceremony hold for a modern European democracy? And, more fundamentally, what does it reveal about the Polish understanding of history, sovereignty, and national identity?

Bolesław Chrobry's coronation in 1025 was not merely a ceremonial investiture; it was a declaration of Poland's sovereignty at a time when the Holy Roman Empire sought to assert dominance over Central Europe. The coronation marked the culmination of Chrobry's decades-long effort to secure Poland's place among the independent kingdoms of Christendom. His status had already been acknowledged by Emperor Otto III, who, during the Congress of Gniezno in 1000, placed his crown upon Chrobry's head in a gesture that some chroniclers misinterpreted as an early coronation. However, it was only in 1025, following the deaths of both Emperor Henry II and Pope Benedict VIII, that Poland could assert its independence unchallenged by external forces.

This act was more than a dynastic milestone; it was the foundation of Polish statehood. By claiming the royal title, Chrobry ensured that Poland would be recognised as a kingdom rather than a mere duchy subservient to imperial authority. From that moment, Poland ceased to be a peripheral Slavic entity and became an equal player in medieval European politics. The significance of this coronation is comparable to the Magna Carta in England or the Declaration of Arbroath in Scotland — a foundational moment affirming a nation's right to self-determination.

Poland has been a republic since 1918, yet the memory of its monarchy has never fully faded. Unlike Britain, where the monarchy remains an enduring institution, Poland saw its kingdom dismantled in 1795 when the country was partitioned by its neighbours and erased from the map of Europe for over a century. Even during that stateless period, Polish national consciousness remained deeply tied to the idea of sovereignty symbolised by the crown. Though the monarchy was abolished, its significance as a unifying force persisted.

A key distinction between the Polish and British monarchies lies in their governing principles. Britain's monarchy has been hereditary, with the crown passing within a single royal lineage over centuries. By contrast, Poland operated under an elective monarchy, particularly during the period of the Polish–Lithuanian Commonwealth (1569–1795). In this system, kings were chosen by the nobility (*szlachta*) rather than inherited through direct descent. This meant that monarchs were often foreigners, elected through complex political negotiations, and bound by constitutional constraints that limited their power. This early experiment in constitutionalism profoundly shaped Polish political identity. Even today, the crowned White Eagle remains Poland's national emblem, a reminder that the state's legitimacy was once symbolised by its monarchy but governed through a collective aristocratic decision rather than dynastic succession.

For many Poles, this anniversary is not about nostalgia for monarchy but about acknowledging the continuity of the Polish state despite its turbulent history. It serves as a reminder that, despite partitions, occupations, and totalitarian rule, Poland has always reclaimed its sovereignty. Celebrating the coronation of the first king is thus an act of historical continuity — a recognition that the Polish state, in its many forms, has endured for a millennium.

To a British reader, whose monarchy has remained an unbroken thread of continuity for over a thousand years, Poland's enthusiasm for commemorating a long-abolished institution might initially seem paradoxical. In Britain, monarchy is a living institution; in Poland, it is a historical anchor. Yet, in both cases, it serves as a symbol of national unity.

Perhaps this difference in perspective explains the initial scepticism of my British interlocutor. In Britain, monarchy represents continuity; in Poland, it symbolises resilience. While the British monarchy evolved gradually over the centuries, adapting to shifting constitutional frameworks, Poland experienced repeated ruptures in its sovereignty. Its history is marked by violent interruptions — partitions, wars, and occupations — which forced the nation to reaffirm its identity repeatedly. For Poland, celebrating the coronation of 1025 is not about restoring a monarchy; it is about reaffirming its right to exist as a sovereign nation, just as it did a thousand years ago.

To celebrate a coronation in a republic may seem paradoxical, but for Poland, it is a profoundly meaningful act. It is not about restoring a bygone system of governance but about recognising the historical milestones that shaped the nation. The millennium of Bolesław Chrobry's coronation is a moment to reflect on Poland's long-standing presence in Europe, its struggles for sovereignty, and its ultimate endurance as a nation-state.

For a country that has faced more than its fair share of existential threats, history is not merely a subject of academic interest but a vital part of national identity. In Poland, history is alive, and the coronation of 1025 is not just a medieval event; it is a symbol of resilience, independence, and the enduring spirit of a nation that has defied the odds for a thousand years.

PART III

LITERATURE AND LEGACY: POLAND'S CULTURAL IMPRINT

The Literary Canon and the Power of Translation: A Polish Perspective

What determines literary immortality? The question of the canon has long been a battlefield for critics, educators, and cultural commentators. At its core, a literary canon is a selection of works deemed essential by generations of readers, scholars, and institutions. It is often viewed as a repository of cultural authority, shaped by historical, political, and social forces. Yet beyond debates on the ideological underpinnings of the canon, there lies a far more pragmatic determinant: translation. For literature written outside the English-speaking world, translation — primarily into English — functions as the gatekeeper to global recognition. The world canon is, in many ways, an Anglo-American construct, determined not by the intrinsic literary value of a work but by the likelihood of its successful transmission across linguistic and cultural boundaries.

To illustrate this, consider Harold Bloom's seminal book *The Western Canon*, a 1994 defence of literary greatness against what he perceived as the encroachment of political correctness. Bloom's pantheon of world literature includes Shakespeare, Cervantes, Milton, Tolstoy, and Proust — figures whose presence in the canon is incontestable. However, when examining his selection of Polish authors, the list appears eccentric: Bruno Schulz, Czesław Miłosz, Witold Gombrowicz, Stanisław Lem, Zbigniew Herbert, and Adam Zagajewski. What unites these names is not merely literary excellence but successful English-language translations at pivotal moments. The absence of Poland's greatest Romantic poet, Adam Mickiewicz, or its most celebrated nineteenth-century novelist, Henryk Sienkiewicz, speaks volumes. If a writer is untranslated — or translated poorly — they remain outside the Anglophone world's literary consciousness.

One might assume that the process of canonisation is organic, driven by readers' appreciation and literary merit. In reality, it is a series of strategic endorsements by translators, publishers, critics, and institutions. The success of Miłosz and Zagajewski, for example, owes much to their translators — figures such as Clare Cavanagh and Stanisław Barańczak — who wield immense influence over how foreign literature is received in the English-speaking world. A competent translator not only renders words into another language but shapes the very perception of an author. The role of translators in establishing a writer's reputation is rarely acknowledged, yet it is often decisive.

Consider the case of Wisława Szymborska. Before winning the Nobel Prize in 1996, her poetry was scarcely known outside Poland. The prize catalysed a surge of interest, but it was the translations by Barańczak and Cavanagh that made her accessible to an international audience. Without these English-language volumes, she would likely have remained a local treasure rather than a global icon. The same applies to the Polish Renaissance poet Jan Kochanowski, whose *Laments* — widely considered one of the great works of early modern European poetry — languished in obscurity until translated by Nobel laureate Seamus Heaney and Stanisław Barańczak. A previous, arguably superior, translation by Adam Czerniawski was largely ignored because it lacked the imprimatur of a major publisher or an influential literary name.

The process of translation is not simply a linguistic exercise; it is a form of literary diplomacy. A book's journey from a national classic to a world masterpiece depends on the interplay of multiple factors: the choice of translator, the prestige of the publisher, the endorsement of critics, and the attention of influential media. Consider *Ferdydurke*, Gombrowicz's absurdist novel, long overlooked until its English translation by Danuta Borchardt, championed by Susan Sontag and published by Yale University Press, secured its place in the world literary conversation. This combination of a skilled translator, a prestigious publishing house, and an intellectual endorsement is what ultimately makes or breaks a writer's reception in the global arena.

Anthologies, too, wield immense power in shaping literary perception. When *The Chicago Review* published a special edition on Polish literature in 1999, its selection of poets — including Miłosz, Herbert, and Zagajewski — effectively dictated who was considered "canonical" in Polish poetry abroad. Similarly, Adam Zagajewski's prominence in American literary circles is partly a result of his academic presence in the United States and his frequent appearances in *The New Yorker* — exposures facilitated by an accessible and eloquent translator.

The implications of this phenomenon extend beyond Poland. The broader reality is that a significant portion of the world's literary heritage remains unknown to Anglophone readers. The dominance of English in publishing, academia, and media means that literature not translated into English is, for all intents and purposes, excluded from the so-called "universal" canon. This raises questions about who curates world literature and how linguistic gatekeeping affects our understanding of global literary history.

If translation is the key to canonisation, what then of the works that are left untranslated, or translated with little care? Literary greatness may be universal in theory, but in practice, it is determined by a series of contingent factors: the right translator at the right time, an influential patron, a receptive literary climate. Without these, even masterpieces remain in the shadows, waiting for the right linguistic passport to admit them into the world's libraries.

In an era where literary borders are more porous than ever, it is worth reconsidering how we define the "universal" canon. The notion that a work's intrinsic quality guarantees its place in the pantheon is a comforting illusion. The reality is far more capricious, dictated by the invisible hands of translators, publishers, and critics. If we are to take the idea of world literature seriously, we must acknowledge that its foundations are not merely aesthetic but profoundly linguistic. The canon, it seems, is not written in stone — it is written in translation.

Polish Nobel Prize Winners —
Were They Really Polish?

When I browse bookshops in London and see the works of Polish Nobel Prize winners displayed, I feel a distinct sense of pride. Since 1996, when Wisława Szymborska was awarded the Nobel Prize in Literature, I have been delighted to see her poetry collections prominently featured. It was at that moment, witnessing her recognition on an international stage, that I began to reflect on what it truly means to be a "Polish" Nobel laureate in literature.

In October 1996, following Wisława Szymborska's receipt of the Nobel Prize, certain Swedish newspapers hailed her as the fifth Polish laureate of this prestigious award. This pronouncement must have surprised many Polish readers, who would have confidently counted her as the fourth, following Henryk Sienkiewicz (1905), Władysław Reymont (1924), and Czesław Miłosz (1980). The discrepancy arose from the inclusion of Isaac Bashevis Singer, whom the Encarta Encyclopaedia described as a "Polish-born American writer in the Yiddish language [who] drew heavily on his Polish background and on the stories of Jewish and medieval European folklore [...]. In 1978 he won the Nobel Prize in Literature for an 'impassioned narrative art' that is rooted in Polish-Jewish culture."

This raises an intriguing question: who, indeed, can be considered a "Polish" Nobel laureate? The issue is far from straightforward. Take, for instance, another case of national ambiguity. A poem by Miłosz, the 1980 Nobel Prize winner, appeared in *The Best American Poetry 1999*, an anthology edited by Robert Bly. Originally written in Polish and first published in Poland in Miłosz's collection *Piesek przydrożny* (*A Road-Side Dog*, 1997), the poem was subsequently translated by the poet himself in collaboration with Robert Hass and reprinted in *The Partisan*

Review. In Poland, there is no doubt that Miłosz was a Polish writer — a political exile who left Poland in 1951, eventually settling in the United States. And yet, for the publisher of this anthology, Miłosz evidently belonged to American literature. His biographical note mentions his Polish connection only in passing: "[After the Second World War he] joined the Polish diplomatic service." As a naturalised American citizen and a professor at the University of California, Berkeley, he was, in this context, an American poet.

It may be justifiable to consider Singer a Jewish-American writer who was born and raised in Poland, and whose works were profoundly influenced by his Polish background, just as it may be reasonable to describe Miłosz as a Polish-American writer born in Lithuania into a Polish-Lithuanian family. However, the official Nobel Prize records list both as American laureates, likely due to their American citizenship at the time of their recognition. This raises further questions: what, ultimately, determines national literary identity? Is it the writer's native language? The language of their literary output? Citizenship? Country of birth? Country of residence? Or is it, perhaps, the cultural milieu that has most fundamentally shaped their work? Should Singer be regarded as Polish, Jewish, or American? Should Miłosz be considered Polish, Lithuanian, or American?

In Poland, both Singer's and Miłosz's Nobel Prizes came as a surprise — not merely because of national ambiguity but because, at the time of their awards, both were relatively unknown in their supposed homeland. In the 1960s and '70s, as Singer's reputation flourished in the United States and Europe, his works remained largely unread in Poland, victims of the Communist regime's antisemitic censorship. Similarly, when Miłosz received the Nobel Prize in 1980, all his works were banned in Poland for political reasons.

The debate over which writers belong on the list of Polish Nobel laureates leads inevitably to a broader question: what constitutes Polish culture? Do all the ethnic groups that lived in the old Polish–Lithuanian Commonwealth fall under its cultural heritage? Singer provides a compelling case study. Writing in Yiddish, he depicted a Jewish community that was self-contained, unassimilated, and deeply rooted in its own traditions and values. Can such a portrayal be considered part of Polish literature? The question of who qualifies as a "Polish writer" is complex. It involves both self-identification and external classification, shaped by political and historical contexts.

Miłosz's literary career can be read as an extended meditation on identity, a reflection on the search for both an earthly and a spiritual homeland by a twentieth-century man born in Central Europe, shaped by two world wars, and caught in the ideological straitjacket of Communism's "historical necessity". His essays and poetry blend reflections on Lithuania, Poland, France, and the United States with metaphysical explorations and meditations on the spiritual legacy of Western civilisation. When he returned to Poland in 1981, greeted as a national hero by the post-Solidarity era, he took pains to resist being cast as an exclusively Polish or exclusively Catholic thinker. When awarded an honorary doctorate by the Catholic University of Lublin — the only university in Poland where his work had been openly discussed prior to 1980 — Miłosz made a pointed statement: "I have never been a Catholic writer." For many Polish readers, this was perplexing. That he wrote in Polish seemed, to them, to preclude any such distancing from his national identity. Yet Miłosz added further complexity by accepting honorary citizenship of independent Lithuania, a move that unsettled some Poles who preferred to remember only his Polish affiliations. The fact that he was born in Lithuania at a time when it was under Russian control, in a region that had once been part of the Polish–Lithuanian Commonwealth, merely added another layer to his already multifaceted identity.

Szymborska, in contrast, presents no such ambiguities. She was a Polish poet who wrote in Polish and lived in Poland. Her status as a Polish Nobel laureate is indisputable. But does such clarity matter? Arguably, it does not. Leading Polish poets of the twentieth century — Zbigniew Herbert, Tymoteusz Karpowicz, Tadeusz Różewicz, Adam Zagajewski, and Miłosz himself — transcend national labels. Their poetry, first and foremost, addresses universal themes. Indeed, Polish poetry finds its greatest resonance abroad not when it is explicitly Polish, but when it speaks to universal human concerns. Consider Miłosz's poem *A Ball*, included in *The Best American Poetry 1999*. The anthology's editors felt no compulsion to underline his Polishness. The same can be said of Herbert and Zagajewski, both of whom publish extensively in the United States. When their poems appear in *The New York Review of Books*, their Polish origins are often an afterthought.

This may be unsettling for Polish readers, yet it is a testament to the fact that Polish poetry has, at last, found its place in the mainstream of world literature. Perhaps, then, the question is not whether these Nobel laureates were "really Polish", but whether, in the grander scheme of literature, such distinctions even matter.

Olga Tokarczuk: Eccentric Truths, Universal Questions

Not long ago, browsing the shelves of Blackwell's in Oxford, I came across a generous display devoted to Olga Tokarczuk. There were all the expected titles: *The Books of Jacob*, *Flights*, *Drive Your Plow Over the Bones of the Dead* — arranged not only as a tribute to a Nobel laureate, but as an invitation to English readers to discover something rare: a writer who is both profoundly Polish and unmistakably European.

Tokarczuk, born in 1962 in the provincial town of Sulechów, writes fiction that travels far beyond Poland's borders — and, for that matter, beyond the usual conventions of narrative. Her novels are often described as "constellation novels", those loose, star-patterned structures that forgo linear storytelling in favour of thematic drift. Her characters, like her readers, are constantly in motion: across continents, time zones, and states of mind.

And yet, for all this cosmopolitanism, she remains deeply rooted in the Polish imagination. *Drive Your Plow Over the Bones of the Dead* — a book that has enjoyed a cult following in Britain — tells the story of Janina Duszejko, an elderly woman living in the Sudeten mountains near the Czech border. Part astrologer, part William Blake devotee, and part amateur sleuth, Janina is the sort of person rural communities often describe as "odd" with a mixture of fear and condescension.

When local hunters start turning up dead, Janina becomes convinced that the animals are taking revenge. This is not, as one might think, a country-house murder mystery with a twist. It's something stranger — and more unsettling. The novel blends comedy, crime, ecological fable, and philosophical meditation into a narrative that feels, at times, like Thomas Bernhard rewritten by a vegan Agatha Christie.

Blake's presence is more than ornamental. The novel's title is lifted from *The Proverbs of Hell*, and Janina translates his poems into Polish with the help of a neighbour. It's a fitting pairing. Both Blake and Tokarczuk write against the grain, rejecting mechanistic reason in favour of vision. And both believe, deeply, in the moral significance of the imagination.

Tokarczuk is a trained psychologist, and her work is shaped by an understanding of the human mind that is neither clinical nor sentimental. Janina, with her conspiracy theories, her unorthodox theology, and her passion for animal rights, is treated with seriousness, not ridicule. What makes the novel remarkable is that we are never quite invited to laugh at her, nor to adopt her worldview entirely. She is both wrong and right, eccentric and prophetic — a walking provocation to the dull certainties of modern life.

British readers, used to crime fiction that either confirms social order or tears it down with flourish, will find *Drive Your Plow* a different proposition. It is a novel of small moments and large implications: about how we treat the non-human world, how we dismiss the elderly, how we prefer order to justice. It asks inconvenient questions, and gives no tidy answers. Unsurprisingly, it has struck a chord. Dua Lipa, no less, has made it the January 2025 pick for her Service95 Book Club, describing it as "a crime novel, but much more than a mere whodunnit" — which is exactly right.

Tokarczuk's international reputation owes much to her translators — Antonia Lloyd-Jones and Jennifer Croft among them — who have rendered her prose into supple, idiomatic English. But it also owes something to the fact that her concerns are, increasingly, our own: ecology, displacement, the nature of belief, the weight of memory.

Flights, her Booker-winning novel, dispenses with plot almost entirely. Instead, it offers a sequence of philosophical fragments: a seventeenth-century anatomist preserving human organs in Amsterdam; a woman who disappears with her child in a Croatian fishing village; a meditation on travel as both escape and confrontation. It is a book that resists summary, and rewards rereading. There is something daring — and oddly consoling — in Tokarczuk's refusal to simplify. The world is complex, she insists, and literature should reflect that.

In Poland, Tokarczuk is admired and attacked in equal measure. Her progressive politics, outspoken feminism, and criticism of nationalism have made her a lightning rod for cultural debate. She has been accused by right-wing politicians of "blackening" Polish history, and has received both standing ovations and death threats. She is, in short, a serious writer — one whose books matter not only to readers but to governments.

Her status as a public intellectual is earned, not assumed. Tokarczuk speaks frequently on environmental issues, democratic backsliding, and the responsibilities of writers in a distracted age. But she does so with the same mixture of clarity and ambiguity that animates her fiction. She is not a pamphleteer. She is a novelist who knows that questions outlive answers.

That her books now occupy prime display space in English bookshops is more than a personal triumph — it is a quiet vindication of Polish literature itself, so often pigeonholed as tragic, historical, or just too distant. Tokarczuk has reminded English readers that Polish writing can be witty, experimental, contemporary — and unashamedly strange.

There is a scene in *Drive Your Plow* where Janina, weary of bureaucracy and human obtuseness, tries to explain the logic of astrology to the police. They, predictably, ignore her. "One day," she says, "people will say that animals were right." It's the kind of line that lingers. Tokarczuk's fiction is full of such moments — half-riddle, half-warning — delivered in prose that glows with intelligence and quiet defiance.

We live in a literary culture that often prefers confession to invention, commentary to craft. Tokarczuk reminds us that fiction can still surprise us, still unsettle us, still move between the stars and the soil. She is a writer who believes, against the odds, that literature can make the world slightly more bearable — not by simplifying it, but by restoring its strangeness.

And that, perhaps, is her greatest gift.

Lord Byron's Second Nation

There are few literary paradoxes as satisfying as that of Lord Byron in Poland. The English, who produced him, have spent two centuries trying to decide whether to take him seriously. The Poles never hesitated.

As a student, I came across Byron's *Euthanasia* in Adam Mickiewicz's translation, and the fascination it sparked has never quite left me. It led to long, circuitous paths through both Polish and English Romanticism, and to one question in particular: why did Poland embrace Byron so thoroughly, so unreservedly, while Britain has always seemed unsure what to make of him? In the modern English canon, Byron holds an uneasy place. He is acknowledged, of course, as one of the major Romantics — but with qualifications. Wordsworth and Keats are treated as the spiritual heavyweights, Coleridge as the metaphysician. Byron is the scandalous aristocrat who wrote long poems and behaved badly on the Continent. He is remembered as much for his waistcoats and lovers as for *Don Juan*.

In Poland, by contrast, Byron was canonised almost immediately. For Adam Mickiewicz — the towering figure of Polish Romanticism — Byron was not merely a literary influence but a moral and political ally, a kindred spirit in the truest Romantic sense. The Byronic hero, exiled, brooding, and defiant, found his natural readership in a country itself cast into exile.

To understand this embrace, one must consider the context. In the early nineteenth century, Poland was not a nation but a memory — its territory partitioned between Russia, Prussia, and Austria. Romanticism, with its cult of the dispossessed hero and its mistrust of tyranny, arrived in Poland not as a fashionable import, but as an ideological necessity. Byron's poetry, with its grandiose despair and political rage, seemed to speak directly to the Polish condition. *Childe Harold, The Giaour, Manfred* — all read in translation, of course, but rarely as mere translation. The texts were absorbed and repurposed. Byron became, in a real sense, Polish.

Mickiewicz did not simply imitate Byron — he remodelled him. In works such as *Konrad Wallenrod* and *Dziady* (*Forefathers' Eve*), Byron's tropes appear in Polish guise: the doomed hero, the sacrificial struggle, the tension between fate and agency. But where Byron's despair often drifted into decadent posturing, Mickiewicz returned again and again to national suffering. His Romanticism was political in a way that Byron's, for all its flair, rarely was. Byron wrote from a position of voluntary exile; Mickiewicz, from enforced absence. One chose to leave; the other could not return.

This distinction mattered little to the thousands of Poles who read Byron as scripture. During the November Uprising of 1830–31, his poetry circulated as quasi-revolutionary text. That he had fought and died for Greek independence gave him even greater moral authority. Byron was not just a poet — he was a symbol: of resistance, of idealism, of Europe's unfinished business. He was, in Polish eyes, the Romantic *sans phrase*.

Back in England, things were rather more complicated. Byron's radical politics — so attractive to oppressed nations — became, over time, a source of discomfort. His contempt for British society, his sneering at institutions, his refusal to behave — none of this endeared him to the Victorian establishment. He was too grandiloquent for the modernists, too unserious for the critics, and too worldly for the mystics. He fell, awkwardly, between traditions. The English admire his wit, quote his epigrams, and keep his works on the syllabus. But they do not quite love him.

In Poland, they did — and do. He was a European figure in a way that his fellow Romantics were not. Shelley was too ethereal, Keats too interior, Wordsworth too rooted in place. Byron belonged to no one landscape. He belonged to the idea of Europe — fractured, wandering, half-mad with hope.

The Polish literary tradition, with its ease at absorbing foreign models, had no trouble with Byron. Mickiewicz's engagement with his work was not a matter of translation, nor even imitation. It was a dialogue. The notion, cherished in English letters, that true originality means writing ex nihilo was largely absent. Polish Romanticism was born in conversation with Europe — not in defiance of it.

Which leads to a broader, more interesting point: at what moment does cultural borrowing become transformation? When Mickiewicz shaped his own Romantic heroes in Byron's image, was he translating, adapting, or creating anew? These are not simply academic questions. They remind us that literary influence is rarely a straight line. It loops, reverses, multiplies. And sometimes, as in this case, it crosses borders so thoroughly that the origin begins to matter less than the outcome.

For me, this remains one of the enduring pleasures of literary history: watching the afterlives of writers evolve in places they never visited. Byron never set foot in Poland. But his words marched there, whispered in uprisings, quoted by exiles, recast by poets. He was more useful to Poland than to England. And in a way, more at home.

Even now, Byron is easier to read in Warsaw than in Oxford. His Romanticism — so unfashionable in its rhetoric, so grand in its tragic postures — feels oddly contemporary in a country still grappling with questions of identity, loss, and defiance. For the English, Byron remains a challenge to categorise. For the Poles, he is an honorary citizen.

Perhaps that is his truest legacy. Not as a poet who belongs to any one nation, but as a figure claimed by those who needed him most. Byron may have died in Missolonghi, but his literary resurrection took place, quite unmistakably, in the lands east of Vienna — in the Polish heartlands where Romanticism became resistance.

A Polish Bard in Shakespeare's Garden

A curious thing happened in Stratford-upon-Avon, that most sacrosanct of literary pilgrimage sites. Amid the Tudor beams and the ever-present whiff of Bardolatry, a statue appeared — not of a minor Elizabethan poet or some overlooked Jacobean dramatist, but of a Polish Renaissance luminary. Jan Kochanowski, a name unfamiliar to most Britons, now stands solemnly in the sculpture garden of Anne Hathaway's Cottage, forever contemplating the ghosts of iambs past. But why would the Poles plant their greatest poet in the hallowed ground of Shakespeare's hometown? What does this say about the deep entanglements of cultural memory, literary admiration, and, dare we say, a touch of national vanity?

The statue was unveiled in June 2022 in a ceremony infused with all the dignity and warmth such an occasion demands. The Polish Cultural Institute in London and the Shakespeare Birthplace Trust collaborated on the event, extolling Kochanowski's virtues and presenting him as Shakespeare's Slavic counterpart. The sculptor, Andrew Lilley, drew inspiration from Kochanowski's most haunting work, *Laments*, a series of elegies mourning the death of his young daughter. That very theme — parental grief — forms an indelible link between the Polish poet and the English playwright, for Shakespeare, too, knew the agony of losing a child. In this shared sorrow, these two Renaissance giants are bound together, a poetic fraternity of the bereaved.

The statue itself is a thing of quiet dignity. Lilley chose to depict Kochanowski not in the grandeur of his poetic triumphs but in the intimate throes of grief, mirroring the lamentation that pulses through his verse. If Shakespeare is forever the impish wordsmith, Kochanowski here is the mourning father, a man for whom no words could quite suffice. The unveiling was accompanied by Tudor music, poetry readings, and even bust-making workshops for children, as though Stratford were eager to extend an olive branch to the legacy of this Polish guest.

The parallels between the two writers extend beyond their tragedies. Both were polymaths of their age, their quills dipped in myriad genres. Shakespeare gave the world histories, comedies, tragedies, and sonnets, while Kochanowski, with equal deftness, composed lyrical poetry, dramas, hymns, and biting satires. If English literature had *Hamlet*, Polish letters had *The Dismissal of the Greek Envoys*, an equally eloquent meditation on political folly and moral decay. And yet, while Shakespeare has enjoyed an almost celestial ascendancy, Kochanowski's renown remains largely provincial, his verses cherished in Poland but rarely travelling far beyond its borders.

One might question, then, whether this tribute in Stratford is a generous act of cultural exchange or a charming instance of Polish ambition. After all, it is one thing to celebrate Shakespeare in Poland — he is the undisputed colossus of world literature — but quite another to place a Polish poet in the garden of England's greatest literary son. Is this not an act of cultural wishful thinking, an attempt to seat Kochanowski at the great banquet of European literature, where Shakespeare presides as an undisputed host?

Yet, to dismiss this as mere megalomania would be unfair. Poland has long venerated Shakespeare, translating and performing his works with a fervour that rivals, if not surpasses, Britain's own. The nation has, in a sense, earned the right to be reciprocated in kind. Kochanowski is not some obscure figure dredged up for the sake of patriotic posturing. He was a true Renaissance master, a literary architect of the Polish language much as Shakespeare was for English. If Poland has accepted Shakespeare as its own, might England not extend the same courtesy?

The placement of Kochanowski's statue in Stratford is thus more than an exercise in cultural diplomacy — it is a reflection of literary kinship. The two poets never met, yet their works resonate across centuries and borders. Both emerged from worlds at once provincial and cosmopolitan, channelling the humanist currents of their time into something uniquely national and yet strikingly universal. In their hands, language became not just a vehicle for expression but a playground for invention. It is fitting, then, that Kochanowski's likeness should now stand in the birthplace of English literature's greatest alchemist.

Of course, the presence of a Polish bard in Stratford may not immediately stir the hearts of British visitors, for whom the name Kochanowski means little. But there is something quietly subversive in his placement — an assertion that great literature is not the sole province of one nation, that the Renaissance spirit flourished in many tongues, in many lands. If nothing else, the statue invites curiosity. Who was this Polish poet, standing with such solemnity in Shakespeare's garden? And might he, too, be worth reading?

Perhaps that is the greatest triumph of this statue — not merely to honour Kochanowski, but to suggest that literature itself is a conversation, an eternal dialogue across time and space. Shakespeare, after all, was never meant to be confined to England, nor Kochanowski to Poland. Both poets belong to all who cherish the play of words, the drama of existence, and the solace of poetry in times of grief. In that sense, Jan Kochanowski's statue is not an intrusion into Stratford's literary landscape, but a welcome expansion of its horizons.

Why *Lalka* Is My Favourite Novel and Why I Enjoy Reading It in London

Bolesław Prus's *Lalka* (*The Doll*) is widely regarded as one of the greatest Polish novels of the nineteenth century. It is a masterpiece of realism, a profound social study, and an intricate psychological portrait of its protagonist, Stanisław Wokulski. The novel captivates me not only because of its rich characterisation and philosophical depth but also because of its remarkable treatment of modernity, commerce, and the struggles of an emerging middle class — themes that resonate even today.

Reading *Lalka* in London provides a unique perspective. The novel, though deeply rooted in Warsaw, has a universal appeal that makes it particularly interesting in an English context. London, like Warsaw in the novel, was undergoing rapid transformations in the late nineteenth century. The tensions between old aristocratic traditions and new commercial ambitions, so vividly depicted in *Lalka*, find strong echoes in Victorian England. Furthermore, there are direct references to England in the novel, which allow for a fascinating comparison between Polish and British societies of the time.

Prus's novel contains several references to England and its influence. One of the most notable aspects is Wokulski's admiration for British industry and scientific progress. Unlike many of his Polish contemporaries, who remained bound to traditional ways, Wokulski recognises the importance of industrialisation and seeks to engage with it. This is evident in his travels to France and England, where he observes the advancements made by Western European nations. His fascination with technological progress reflects the aspirations of an ambitious entrepreneur striving to bridge the gap between the underdeveloped Polish lands and the modern industrial world. The character of Julian Ochocki, an inventor and scientist, also embodies the admiration for British progress. He represents the idealistic scientist who believes in the transformative power of technology — an attitude reminiscent of many British industrialists and inventors of the Victorian era. His belief in science and industry aligns with the spirit of innovation that defined nineteenth-century Britain. Moreover, the novel references English goods and commodities, highlighting the high regard in which British products were held in Poland. British fashion, textiles, and other manufactured goods were viewed as symbols of modernity and quality. This aligns with how Victorian England was perceived in continental Europe as a model of economic and industrial success.

One of the most striking comparisons between *Lalka* and British literature is its resemblance to the novels of Charles Dickens. Like Dickens, Prus explores themes of social mobility, economic struggles, and the moral dilemmas faced by individuals caught between different social classes. Stanisław Wokulski's journey from a poor background to a successful businessman bears similarities to the trajectories of many Dickensian protagonists, such as Pip from *Great Expectations*. Both characters strive for a higher social standing and believe that financial success will enable them to achieve personal fulfilment. However, while Pip eventually learns the emptiness of social ambition, Wokulski remains tragically caught between his desires and the rigid structures of Polish society.

Additionally, Prus, like Dickens, is a master of depicting urban life. Just as Dickens captures the bustling energy and social disparities of London, Prus portrays Warsaw with the same meticulous attention to detail. The descriptions of Warsaw's streets, businesses, and cafés create a vivid image of a city in flux, where different social groups coexist yet remain deeply divided. This sense of a changing metropolis, with its opportunities and constraints, is something that a London reader can immediately recognise and appreciate. Yet, *Lalka* differs from Dickensian novels in its philosophical and psychological depth. While Dickens often provides clear moral resolutions, Prus leaves his characters in a state of ambiguity. Wokulski's ultimate fate remains uncertain, and his struggles with love, ambition, and societal constraints reflect the existential dilemmas faced by many individuals in an era of rapid change. This makes *Lalka* not just a social novel but also a profound psychological and philosophical study.

Living in London while reading *Lalka* enhances the experience of the novel. London, much like nineteenth-century Warsaw, is a city of contrasts — a place where history coexists with modernity, where wealth and poverty exist side by side, and where social mobility is both possible and yet often constrained by invisible barriers. The novel's themes of ambition, class struggle, and the tension between tradition and progress are as relevant in contemporary London as they were in nineteenth-century Warsaw. Furthermore, London's Victorian architecture, its historical bookstores, and its literary heritage provide the perfect backdrop for engaging with a novel from the same era. Walking through the streets of Bloomsbury or Mayfair, one can almost imagine Wokulski himself, a man caught between the past and the future, wandering through these same streets, contemplating his next move.

For English-speaking readers interested in *Lalka*, a translation by David Welsh is available, published by Central European University Press. The translation captures the essence of Prus's prose, ensuring that the novel's richness and depth are preserved. I highly recommend *Lalka* to English readers who enjoy Dickens, Balzac, or Tolstoy. It is a novel that combines the social realism of Dickens, the psychological insights of Dostoevsky, and the historical depth of Tolstoy. It is not just a Polish novel — it is a European novel, a universal story of human ambition, love, and disillusionment. Reading *Lalka* offers a unique opportunity to step into nineteenth-century Warsaw and explore the intricate social fabric of the time. For those living in London, the experience is even more rewarding, as it invites comparisons with Victorian England and allows the reader to see how themes of social mobility, ambition, and change transcend national borders. In an era where classic literature is being rediscovered and reinterpreted, *Lalka* deserves a place alongside the great novels of European realism. It is a book that speaks to the heart and mind, reminding us of the timeless struggles between love and ambition, tradition and progress. For anyone looking for a novel that is both intellectually stimulating and emotionally engaging, *Lalka* is an excellent choice.

A Polish Eye on England's Harbours
— with Joseph Conrad in Mind

One of the peculiarities of diplomatic life is its temporal dislocation — forever present, yet never quite at home. We drift through cities like attentive ghosts, noting the details others overlook. That feeling sharpens in England's port towns. Not because of the sea alone, but because of one Pole who made it a metaphor for human complexity.

Joseph Conrad — born Józef Teodor Konrad Korzeniowski in the landlocked reaches of what is now Ukraine — spent much of his life moored in English harbours: Lowestoft, Tilbury, Gravesend. He gazed at the oceans he would sail, but also inward, to the murkier depths where only fiction could sound the moral line.

English came late to him, yet he mastered it with such poise and gravity that he became, in some eyes, more English than the English. His sensibility, though, remained unmistakably Central European — ironic, historically conscious, and drawn to questions of honour, fate, and fractured identity.

For diplomats, an affinity with Conrad is all but inevitable. Like him, we set off in search of broader horizons. Like him, we interpret foreign manners and mumbled codes, sensing meanings that don't sit neatly on the surface. Conrad's England — welcoming yet withholding — must have struck him as a puzzle, as it often does for those of us who speak plainly but think in other registers.

Not long ago, during a rare pause from official life, I visited Southampton. The town wore a melancholy typical of English weather: grey drizzle on grey stone, streets subdued, buildings quietly enduring. At the docks, I tried to see Southampton as Conrad might have — less as a setting than a state of mind. Not simply a place of departure and return, but of reckoning. Ships here bore more than cargo; they carried questions unresolved and burdens unspoken.

Conrad understood ports as thresholds: not merely between land and sea, but between law and lawlessness, civilisation and its discontents. In his fiction, London and Bristol became zones of moral tension, places where empire and solitude met in uneasy truce. His Thames in *Heart of Darkness* is not just a river, but a route "into the uttermost ends of the earth", and beyond that, into something far less charted.

From Southampton, I made my way east, eventually arriving in Canterbury, where Conrad lies with his wife Jessie beneath a modest headstone in the city's quiet cemetery. Unlike the port towns that shaped his maritime imagination, Canterbury rests inland, removed from the tide's reach. And yet, standing there, I sensed no rupture. The stillness of the place echoed something deeper in Conrad's fiction — not the call of departure, but the weight of return. His journey ended far from the sea, but the questions he posed still drift beneath the surface.

My interest in these towns is not just historical. It's about temperament. These places — Hull, Liverpool, Plymouth — still look outward, as they always have. Not because someone tells them to, but because memory has shaped their gaze. And memory, as Conrad knew, is never tidy. The sea brought trade and power, but also conquest, suffering, unease. He never moralised, never offered the reader a clean conscience. Innocence, for him, was always fragile — often deluded.

At Portsmouth, standing before HMS *Victory*, I recalled Conrad's belief that honour is not a posture but a discipline. His Lord Jim is felled not by treachery but by a single moment of fear. To modern ears, the word *honour* may sound faintly antique — suited to costume dramas and retired colonels. But to Conrad, and to those of us shaped by Central Europe's ironic legacy, it remains stubbornly vital.

Diplomacy, after all, is a balancing act between urgency and restraint. We live by silences — some honourable, some evasive, some simply fearful. Conrad understood this better than most. His fiercest storms were never at sea, but in the soul.

There is no need to sentimentalise the past. Seen through Polish eyes, these ports are not relics of lost grandeur, but reminders that identity is never fixed. Conrad became English in language and livelihood, but his moral imagination remained unmistakably Polish — shaped by a culture steeped in irony, endurance, and ethical introspection. His surroundings changed; his inner compass did not.

If these coastal wanderings have taught me anything, it is that horizons are never static. They beckon — or they warn. Conrad faced the unknown not with certainty, but with courage. His stories still unsettle us, still ask the questions we'd rather avoid.

And so, standing in these harbours, I find not nostalgia, but instruction. Conrad's legacy is not a monument but a challenge: to speak plainly, to think deeply, and to move forward without illusions. He left us not answers, but a way of seeing — and that, I suspect, is the more enduring gift.

PART IV

FAITH, THOUGHT, AND THE CROSSROADS OF IDEAS

Ioannes Dantiscus: A Renaissance Envoy in Henry VIII's England

When I arrived in London in 2022 as Poland's Ambassador to the Court of St James's, I was unaware that I was following in the footsteps of an illustrious predecessor. It was Professor Norman Davies, the eminent historian, who, during my *vin d'honneur*, pointed out that exactly five centuries earlier, in 1522, Ioannes Dantiscus had landed in England as an envoy of King Sigismund I the Old to Henry VIII. This, he informed me with his characteristic wit, was the first recorded instance of a Polish diplomat setting foot on English soil. Inspired by this revelation, we later organised a panel at the Warburg Institute — where I had been a visiting fellow in the 1990s — to discuss the significance of Dantiscus's mission.

Dantiscus, or Jan Dantyszek to give him his Polish name, was a man of many talents: poet, humanist, diplomat, bishop, and adventurer. Born in 1485 in Gdańsk, he embodied the spirit of the Polish Renaissance, a period when the Kingdom of Poland was not only a formidable European power but also a hub of intellectual and artistic ferment. His diplomatic service under King Sigismund I took him across Europe, forging connections with rulers, scholars, and artists. Yet, his sojourn in England remains a fascinating episode in his career, offering a window into the interplay of power and diplomacy in the early sixteenth century.

In 1522, Dantiscus's mission was part of Poland's broader strategy to navigate the tumultuous waters of European politics. With the Holy Roman Empire and France locked in bitter rivalry, and England entangled in its own continental ambitions, Sigismund sought to bolster Poland's position by exploring new alliances. Dantiscus, already an experienced diplomat, was dispatched to Henry VIII's court with letters of introduction from the Holy Roman Emperor Charles V and Margaret of

Austria. He set sail from Antwerp, enduring stormy seas before finally arriving in the Kentish port of Sandwich. From there, he travelled to Canterbury, pausing to visit the shrine of St Thomas Becket — a diplomatic nod, perhaps, to England's ecclesiastical traditions — before making his way to London.

His audience with Henry VIII was, by all accounts, a splendid affair. England's young and ambitious monarch was in his prime, exuding the confidence that would later make him infamous across Christendom. Dantiscus described Henry as charismatic and affable, surrounded by the glittering pageantry of the Tudor court. He was also granted an audience with Cardinal Thomas Wolsey, the true power behind the throne and the architect of England's foreign policy. The discussions, while diplomatic in nature, underscored Poland's role as a key player in European affairs, despite its geographical distance from the British Isles.

Dantiscus's correspondence from this period provides a treasure trove of observations, from the elaborate court ceremonies to the peculiarities of English customs. He noted, with a mixture of admiration and bemusement, the formality of English diplomatic protocols and the grandeur of courtly entertainment. His letters, written in the refined Latin of the Renaissance, capture the intellectual curiosity and sharp political insight that defined his career. He was, after all, not merely a diplomat but a scholar, engaging in discussions with leading humanists of his age.

After two months in England, Dantiscus returned to the Continent, his mission complete. His career, however, was far from over. He went on to serve as Poland's envoy to the court of Charles V, earning a reputation as one of the most erudite and effective diplomats of his time. Eventually, he was appointed Bishop of Warmia and devoted his later years to scholarly pursuits. Yet, his encounter with Henry VIII remains a symbolic moment in the long history of Polish-British relations — a testament to Poland's enduring presence on the European stage.

Why, one might ask, should we remember Dantiscus today? Firstly, his journey highlights Poland's deep historical connections with Western Europe, countering the persistent misconception that Poland was somehow peripheral to the grand narrative of European history. In reality, sixteenth-century Poland was a major power, a kingdom that stood at the crossroads of East and West, engaging in diplomacy, trade, and intellectual exchange with the leading states of the time.

Secondly, Dantiscus's legacy reminds us of the enduring importance of diplomacy. In an era when the world was changing rapidly — with the Protestant Reformation on the horizon and the first stirrings of global exploration — envoys like Dantiscus played a crucial role in maintaining dialogue between nations. His meticulous letters, now digitised in the *Corpus Dantiscum* project, remain a valuable source for historians seeking to understand the intricate web of Renaissance diplomacy.

Lastly, there is something inherently appealing about the figure of Dantiscus himself. He was, in many ways, a quintessential Renaissance man — cosmopolitan, multilingual, equally at ease in the courts of kings and the salons of scholars. His life was one of movement and adaptation, qualities that are no less relevant in today's world of shifting alliances and geopolitical uncertainties.

When I reflect on that conversation with Norman Davies in 2022, I am struck by the delightful symmetry of history. Five centuries apart, two Polish diplomats arrived in London, each seeking to strengthen the ties between their homeland and Britain. While much has changed since Dantiscus's time, the fundamental principles of diplomacy — dialogue, mutual respect, and cultural exchange — remain constant. His journey serves as a reminder that history is not merely a series of distant events but a living continuum, shaping the present as much as it illuminates the past.

Bridging Kingdoms: Britain and Poland in the Age of Faith

By all accounts, sixteenth-century Poland and Britain should not have had much to say to one another. One was a kingdom edging towards imperial ambition, still bruised from the Tudors' break with Rome; the other, a vast and fractious Commonwealth of nobles and bishops, celebrated for its toleration as much as its instability. Yet, as Mirosława Hanusiewicz-Lavallee's impressive new study, *The Call of Albion: Protestants, Jesuits, and British Literature in Poland–Lithuania, 1567–1775* (Brill, 2024), makes clear, the confessional dramas that played out between Canterbury and Kraków were anything but marginal. They were lively, often combative, and surprisingly reciprocal.

We tend to imagine early modern Europe as a patchwork of linguistic and religious enclaves. Hanusiewicz-Lavallee's book cuts across that, revealing a brisk intellectual and literary trade between the British Isles and the Polish–Lithuanian Commonwealth. This was not just diplomacy or diaspora (though there was plenty of both), but something subtler and more enduring: the exchange of polemics, translations, adaptations, and — perhaps most intriguingly — literary sympathies.

The story begins, as many such stories do, with persecution. As English Catholics fled Elizabethan England, some found an unlikely sanctuary in Polish cities like Kraków and Braniewo. Jesuits there welcomed them not just as co-religionists, but as living proof of Protestant tyranny. In turn, Polish Catholics read accounts of English martyrs — real, exaggerated, and imagined — with avidity. Jesuit printers translated and disseminated English Catholic literature not out of mere curiosity but to warn of what might come should Protestantism take deeper root at home.

Yet it was not a one-way street. While English Catholic texts were quietly circulating in Polish Catholic seminaries, Polish Protestants were looking westward with equal interest. They found in England's embattled Calvinists and heroic martyrs kindred spirits. One of the more remarkable outcomes was a Polish translation — partial, but enthusiastic — of John Foxe's *Book of Martyrs*, the Protestant hagiography par excellence. The translator, Cyprian Bazylik, adapted Foxe's Latin version into Polish, repurposing its tales of suffering not to glorify Protestant England but to serve Polish Calvinist ends.

Such literary retooling is at the heart of Hanusiewicz-Lavallee's argument. English texts were not imported wholesale, but reinterpreted, redacted, and re-anchored in the shifting sands of Polish confessional politics. This was not imitation; it was strategic domestication. Translation was never merely linguistic. Every theological clause, every rhetorical flourish was recalibrated for a new audience. English martyrs could be Polish ones too — so long as their suffering could be made to speak to local anxieties.

And then there is the remarkable story of *The Pilgrim's Progress*. Bunyan's Puritan allegory might seem an unlikely candidate for Polish readership, and yet a version did appear — filtered through the Calvinist diaspora in Brandenburg-Prussia, delicately shaved of its more strident sectarianism. That such a work could travel across such doctrinal and linguistic divides is testament to literature's curious ability to both cross and preserve boundaries.

Not everything translated so easily. King James I, that most self-regarding of monarchs, features early in the book in a rather less flattering Polish light. A Kraków printing of a Jesuit polemic — almost certainly written by one Kasper Sawicki, though published under a pseudonym — described James as a reeking heretic, unworthy of Christian company. The English ambassador protested; the book was ceremonially burnt in

Kraków's market square. Copies survived, of course. One in Elbląg bears furious marginalia, likely written by an English Catholic émigré. Even then, the Reformation had created unlikely bedfellows.

What becomes clear throughout *The Call of Albion* is that the intellectual corridor between Poland and Britain was paved not with diplomatic niceties, but with theology. The Society of Jesus looms large, as does the figure of Cardinal Stanisław Hosius — both instrumental in shaping the Polish reception of English recusant literature. For Protestants, meanwhile, English polemicists such as John Knox and John Jewel became familiar names in the print shops of Vilnius and Raków.

George Buchanan, the Scottish poet and Protestant firebrand, makes a rather more elegant appearance. His humanist paraphrase of the Psalms inspired the Polish poet Jan Kochanowski, who adapted the form into vernacular verse. Another Buchanan work, the tragedy *Jephthes*, was rendered into Polish by Jan Zawicki — not as a Calvinist lament, but as a Stoic meditation on reason and religious violence. In both cases, Buchanan's words were put to work in very Polish ways.

A similar fate befell John Owen, the prolific English epigrammatist whose Latin couplets were all the rage in early modern Europe. His pithy verses, by turns devout, salacious, and scathing, were translated, paraphrased, and taught across the Jesuit colleges of the Commonwealth. Not everyone was pleased. Some Catholic commentators found Owen's jabs at the papacy rather too pointed for comfort. But others — perhaps admiring the elegance of the barb more than its target — allowed his work to flourish.

What does all this tell us? That the religious history of Europe was not only a matter of creeds and councils, but of books and readers. Poland and Britain may have stood on opposite ends of the confessional divide, but they shared a belief in literature as a weapon in the wars of faith. Jesuits and

Calvinists alike understood that a well-timed translation — or a cleverly repackaged polemic — could do as much as any bishop or ambassador.

And while Hanusiewicz-Lavallee's study is grounded in careful archival work, its implications are quietly profound. It reminds us that influence is not always linear. British texts were reimagined in Poland not because of admiration for England per se, but because of what they could be made to mean in a different context. In a Europe where faith was political and literature theological, the act of reading was itself an intervention.

This is not a story of ecumenism. It is a story of appropriation, misunderstanding, and — more rarely — genuine intellectual engagement. It is a tale of Jesuits who read English Protestant tracts in order to better refute them, and Polish Calvinists who turned English martyrs into local heroes. It is about the strange afterlives of texts, and the quiet power of translation to remake the world.

One leaves *The Call of Albion* with a sense not just of how ideas travel, but of how they adapt — sometimes politely, often polemically — to new terrains. In an age where identity, nationhood, and belief were up for grabs, literature moved in curious ways. England and Poland were never neighbours, but in the libraries and lecture halls of Vilnius and Gdańsk, in the margins of dog-eared volumes, they occasionally spoke the same language.

And that, Hanusiewicz-Lavallee suggests, is worth remembering. Albion called. And someone, somewhere along the Vistula, answered.

Socinianism: Poland's Radical Reformation and Its Anglo-American Echoes

In the Michaelmas term of 1988, I arrived at St Anne's College, Oxford, as a young visiting scholar with a clear academic mission: to immerse myself in the Latin verse of Clementius Ianitius (Klemens Janicki), a now-forgotten Polish poet who once held court among the obscure footnotes of Renaissance literature. My plan was firm. My topic was fixed. But Oxford, in its usual way, had other ideas.

What I found instead, tucked quietly into the college library's holdings, was something altogether more arresting: a shelf of volumes on Socinianism — a movement I had only vaguely associated with the more eccentric margins of the Reformation. Titles like *Socinianism in Seventeenth-Century England* by Herbert John McLachlan and George Hunston Williams's sprawling *The Polish Brethren* offered a door into a lost world of theological radicalism, intellectual daring, and polished polemic. Three years later, my doctoral thesis would not be on Ianitius at all, but on Erazm Otwinowski, a fiery Polish Socinian whose writings are still unnervingly relevant when it comes to matters of faith, reason, and the limits of tolerance.

Socinianism remains one of the most remarkable, and most neglected, episodes in the history of the European Reformation. Flourishing in the Polish–Lithuanian Commonwealth from the late sixteenth century until the mid-seventeenth, it represented Protestantism's radical flank — a movement that not only questioned the Trinity but re-examined the very underpinnings of Christian orthodoxy. Original sin, predestination, the divinity of Christ, the atonement — all were calmly rethought, weighed against reason and Scripture, and, more often than not, found wanting.

The Polish Brethren — as they called themselves, rather more modestly — were not anarchists in cassocks. Their project was disciplined, intellectually rigorous, and rooted in the belief that Christianity could and should make sense. They rejected theological mystery in favour of plain reason. They insisted that the Sermon on the Mount was more than poetic uplift; it was a moral programme. Their epicentre was Raków, a modest town which housed a printing press, a famous academy, and some of the sharpest minds of the age. For a brief but incandescent period, Raków was Geneva without the dourness — Reformation thinking at its most open and its least vengeful.

The death of Jan Łaski (or John a Lasco, as he is better known in the Anglophone world) in 1560 left Polish Calvinism in flux. Into that vacuum stepped men like Giorgio Biandrata and Fausto Sozzini (Latinised, inevitably, as Socinus), whose theological acrobatics left the rest of Europe somewhere between baffled and outraged. They were the sort of Christians who not only doubted the Trinity but wrote books explaining why it was both unbiblical and irrational. The reaction from Rome was predictably ferocious, but the Lutherans and Calvinists were hardly more accommodating.

And yet, for several decades, Poland remained what it had long prided itself on being: a safe haven for religious oddities and intellectual dissenters. While the rest of Europe busied itself with wars of religion, the Commonwealth — courtesy of its notorious *Henrician Articles* and an entrenched culture of aristocratic libertarianism — offered breathing space. Socinians debated, published, and educated. They attracted admirers from abroad. They championed religious toleration before it was fashionable — and long before it was safe.

It could not last. The Counter-Reformation arrived with Jesuit precision, and the noose tightened. In 1638, the Raków Academy was shut down. In 1658, the Brethren were officially expelled. Many fled to the Netherlands, some to Prussia, and a few to England, where their influence would prove surprisingly tenacious. Exile, in their case, became dissemination.

In England, the seventeenth century was a time of confessional volatility and fertile discontent. Socinian books slipped across the Channel, sometimes under false covers, and found their way into the libraries — and imaginations — of English dissenters. John Biddle, often dubbed the father of English Unitarianism, was accused of spreading Socinian heresies with rather too much enthusiasm. In 1648, Parliament felt obliged to ban Socinianism outright — an oddly flattering tribute, given how few English MPs could have located Raków on a map.

But ideas are hard to ban. Socinian thought percolated into the bloodstream of English radicalism. Its fingerprints can be seen in the writings of William Penn, the Quaker founder of Pennsylvania; and in the slow but inexorable rise of English Unitarianism in the eighteenth and nineteenth centuries. The emphasis on rational faith, ethical Christianity, and individual conscience owed a quiet but enduring debt to the Polish Brethren.

Across the Atlantic, the Socinian spirit resurfaced — rebranded, perhaps, but unmistakable. William Ellery Channing's famous Baltimore Sermon of 1819, in which he laid out the core principles of American Unitarianism, would not have startled a Polish theologian of 1605. His rejection of Trinitarian dogma, his belief in human perfectibility, and his cool insistence on reason over mystery all echoed the Brethren. Even Thomas Jefferson, no churchgoer, bore their imprint: his *Jefferson Bible*, stripped of miracles and metaphysics, is Socinianism in all but name.

Why dwell on a defunct sect whose academy was shuttered before the English Civil War even began? Because their questions remain ours. The compatibility of faith and reason. The meaning of tolerance in a world increasingly allergic to it. The ethics of dissent. The Socinians may have debated the Trinity, but their deeper concern was how to live truthfully in an age of violent opinion. That remains an urgent question.

In many ways, the Jesuit–Socinian polemics of the seventeenth century resemble our own ideological battles. Each side believed it held not just the truth, but the sole moral right to speak it. The debates were sharp, and not always scholarly. Rhetoric outpaced charity. Misrepresentation was common. Reading these exchanges now, one is struck by how modern they feel — not in content, but in tone. The sense that error is intolerable, that compromise is betrayal, that one's opponent is not only wrong but dangerous — these are not new habits.

As I discovered in that library at St Anne's more than thirty years ago, Socinianism is not just a curious footnote in Polish religious history. It is a mirror. It reflects our enduring struggle to balance belief and reason, conviction and civility. What began for me as a scholarly detour became an intellectual adventure — one that took me from sixteenth-century Poland to Enlightenment Boston, with stops in Cromwell's London and Jefferson's Virginia.

The Polish Brethren are long gone. Their books survive in rare collections; their academy is a historical site; their influence, mostly unspoken, lives on in the margins of liberal theology. But their questions remain. And in times like ours, that may be the most radical legacy of all.

Erasmus, Holbein, and the
Art of Quiet Revolution

*Dedicated to Grantley McDonald in appreciation of his lucid
scholarship and quiet precision, and in gratitude for a friendship
grounded in shared pursuits — textual criticism, early modern
polemics, and the spirit of Erasmus.*

There are few better places in London to stage a conversation
with history than the National Gallery. One moves from saints
to merchants, monarchs to mythologies, all arranged with
curatorial diplomacy. But it is in Room 4, among the early
Netherlandish works, that a quieter presence waits: Hans
Holbein the Younger's 1523 portrait of Desiderius Erasmus.

It is a painting one does not so much admire as submit to.
Erasmus sits turned slightly to the left, caught mid-thought,
his pen poised delicately above parchment, his gaze fixed on
something — or someone — just beyond the viewer's reach. The
face is familiar from dozens of prints, but Holbein adds weight
and silence to the man. This is not the Erasmus of caricature or
satire, but the scholar as still point in a moving world.

I first stood before this painting in my early days as a young
Renaissance scholar, newly arrived in London from Poland.
Then, as now, I was drawn not only to the subject but to the
quiet assertion the portrait makes: that ideas matter, and that
books are not merely objects but tools of renovation. It is a
conviction Erasmus shared, and which Holbein renders in the
calm confidence of his sitter.

Erasmus, of course, was a master of many forms: satirist,
theologian, textual critic, and the most tireless correspondent of
his age. He moved with ease across the patchwork of sixteenth-
century Europe, teaching in Paris, writing in Basel, advising
princes in Bruges, and exchanging letters with humanists in
Kraków. He was everywhere and nowhere — a cleric without

a benefice, a reformer without a pulpit, a Dutchman without a country.

In England, he is remembered — when he is remembered at all — as a friend of Thomas More and John Colet, a lodger at Queens' College, Cambridge, and the author of *The Praise of Folly*, a work that remains, even now, more mischievous than many academics care to admit. It was Erasmus who gave English humanism its first true momentum, slipping wit and irony into the cracks of scholastic solemnity.

But Poland, too, knew Erasmus well. His letters to Jan Łaski — bishop, reformer, cousin of the more famous (at least in England) John a Lasco — reveal a shared appetite for moral clarity and ecclesiastical reform. "Polonia mea est," Erasmus once wrote, and it was not mere flattery. The Polish Renaissance, too often a footnote in Western accounts, was built on the same classical foundations he promoted: a belief in the civic purpose of education, the value of ancient wisdom, and the possibility — however faint — of reasoned religion.

Holbein's portrait captures all this without ceremony. The scholar's hands rest lightly on a manuscript; the sleeves of his fur-lined robe ripple with restrained luxury. A Renaissance pilaster anchors the background, a nod to the classical order Erasmus spent his life interpreting. And then there is the inscription, sly and elegant: "I am Johannes Holbein, whom it is easier to criticise than to emulate." Whether penned by Erasmus or not, it suggests a mutual respect between subject and artist — each a master of form, each aware of his posterity.

To view this painting today, as a Polish scholar and diplomat long based in London, is to be reminded that humanism, in its best sense, is a transnational inheritance. Erasmus spoke Latin; his readers, from Kraków to Cambridge, replied in the same, though they lived and thought in Polish, French, German, or English. The lines of division — national, doctrinal, political — were real, but so were the bridges. Holbein painted Erasmus in

Basel; the canvas now hangs in London; and it echoes still in minds shaped by both Oxford and Kraków.

Of Erasmus's works, it is *Novum Instrumentum Omne*, his 1516 Greek edition of the New Testament, that carries the heaviest freight. By returning to the original texts — by bypassing the Vulgate, and in some cases correcting it — Erasmus unleashed a revolution disguised as a footnote. Luther would later claim him as a forerunner; Catholics treated him with wary indulgence. Erasmus, typically, preferred neither camp. He longed for reform but feared rupture, wanted clarity but recoiled from violence. In the theological bar-fight of the sixteenth century, he stood awkwardly to the side, muttering about civility.

His other writings, though less incendiary, are no less enduring. *The Education of a Christian Prince* remains a small masterpiece of political ethics — half advice manual, half moral plea. *The Complaint of Peace* reads today like a lost editorial from a vanished age of internationalism: earnest, elegant, and doomed to be ignored. Even his marginalia — caustic, humane, always learned — are worth reading. Erasmus did not found a church. But he helped preserve the idea that churches ought to be intelligible.

Holbein, for his part, offers no halo. There is no saintliness in this image, only seriousness. The light falls gently across Erasmus's forehead, catching the lines of thought and time. His eyes are clear, but not forgiving. This is a man who has seen too much stupidity dressed up as piety, too many swords drawn in the name of peace.

And so, standing before the portrait, I do not feel nostalgia. I feel alignment. Erasmus was not perfect. He was cautious, sometimes evasive, often priggish. But he believed, as perhaps we must again, that books can mend things, that conversation is preferable to crusade, and that learning is a form of virtue. That is not a bad creed.

In an age where opinion is loud and learning often performative, Erasmus remains quietly subversive. He worked in footnotes and forged alliances through syntax. He mistrusted certitude, distrusted slogans, and kept his sense of humour intact. He would not thrive on Twitter.

And yet his presence lingers — in libraries, in margins, in Holbein's calm portrait. He is the scholar who chose thought over dogma, the reformer who preferred correction to rupture. And as I leave the National Gallery, I do so not with the impression of having visited the past, but of having spoken, briefly, with someone who still understands the future.

Holbein's Quiet Duel: More, Cromwell, and the Reformation in Two Faces

It is one of the more quietly theatrical arrangements in any museum: at the Frick Collection in New York, Sir Thomas More and Thomas Cromwell face one another across a grand mantelpiece, neither man blinking, both eternally composed. Hans Holbein the Younger painted both portraits, though not with this confrontation in mind. Yet placed like this — More on the left, Cromwell on the right — the effect is uncanny. It is as if the Reformation itself has been set to canvas, paused mid-argument.

As a Polish observer — one from a country whose own flirtation with Protestant reform was eventually outpaced by an energetic Catholic revival — I find England's Reformation all the more absorbing. Where we reversed course, England doubled down. What better way to consider the matter than through Holbein, a painter whose gift was not only in likeness but in implication?

More, painted in 1527, appears in three-quarter profile, dressed with studied humanist elegance. His fur collar is thick, his gaze alert but inward. There is warmth in the eyes, but also melancholy — the kind that comes from understanding too much. Five years later, Holbein's portrait of Cromwell offers a different tone entirely: frontal, controlled, bureaucratic. Where More invites, Cromwell inspects. The clothing is plainer, the hands more rigid. The room is colder.

Holbein's genius lies in restraint. There is no obvious allegory here, no flailing gestures or theological props. And yet the portraits are dense with meaning. More, the Catholic martyr, was canonised for refusing to bend to Henry VIII's demands. Cromwell, architect of the English Reformation, did most of the bending for him. Their political divergence ended in familiar Tudor fashion: execution for both, just six years apart.

In the National Portrait Gallery in London, copies of these same portraits hang once more — this time as part of *Hans Holbein Re-made*, a quietly brilliant exhibition exploring the legacy of Holbein's court imagery. These early seventeenth-century replicas, some attributed to Holbein's workshop or followers, are part of the *Making Art in Tudor Britain* project, which reads Holbein not just as painter but as brand. The copies differ in brushstroke and atmosphere, but the essential tension remains.

This duel in oil — More and Cromwell staring each other down across centuries — invites more than biographical speculation. It is about the very shape of political conscience. More clung to a moral law higher than any king's command. Cromwell served the moment, shaping England's ecclesiastical independence with legal cunning and evangelical ambition. Both men were devout; both ended headless. One man's martyr is another's obstacle.

For English viewers, these portraits speak to a foundational schism: the birth of Anglicanism, the displacement of Rome, the assertion of sovereign authority in matters spiritual. For Poles, the resonance is different. The Polish–Lithuanian Commonwealth, that sprawling union of noble liberties and Catholic resilience, welcomed the Reformation with interest but ultimately chose Rome with vigour. Lutherans, Calvinists, Socinians — they flourished briefly under the Warsaw Confederation of 1573, which enshrined religious tolerance in law. But the Jesuits returned with counterarguments (and education), and by the mid-seventeenth century, Poland was once again unmistakably Catholic.

That divergence — between England's permanent Protestantism and Poland's Counter-Reformation comeback — gives Holbein's portraits an added layer of intrigue. They are not only images of two men at odds, but symbols of two possible futures. One path led to the King's supremacy, the other to the Pope's. Each choice had its martyrs, its poetry, its politics.

What makes Holbein's work endure is that he understood character as fate. More's eyes carry not just intelligence but foreboding. Cromwell's lips, thin and pressed, suggest someone for whom clarity was a higher virtue than kindness. These are not caricatures. They are, as much as paint can manage, whole people. The art lies in what's not said.

There is, too, something instructive in the way these portraits have been copied, curated, and displayed over the centuries. That curators still place them opposite one another is telling. It is not just historical irony; it is aesthetic argument. They work as a diptych, however unintended — a Reformation in miniature, framed and varnished.

Holbein, a German who became court painter to a country in spiritual flux, had no need to choose sides. He painted Erasmus, Anne Boleyn, Henry VIII, Jane Seymour, and More with equal precision and psychological weight. His portraits were not flattery but records. Even now, they speak with quiet authority.

What these images remind us — whether in New York, London, or Warsaw — is that belief and power are rarely cleanly separated. In both England and Poland, the sixteenth century was not merely a time of theological debate, but of institutional reckoning. And the arts, as Holbein shows, were part of that reckoning. They did not just illustrate events; they shaped them.

More and Cromwell continue to live in popular imagination, thanks in part to Hilary Mantel and Robert Bolt, whose portraits in fiction and film have made these men familiar once more. Yet it is Holbein who gives them permanence. He does not interpret; he reveals. Through him, we do not merely learn about More's scruples or Cromwell's strategy — we feel them.

To stand before these portraits is to confront two ways of being in the world: one anchored in principle, the other in power. Both, of course, proved vulnerable to the axe. But their faces endure. Holbein saw to that.

And from the vantage point of a country that travelled its own path through Reformation and Counter-Reformation, the effect is sobering. We are reminded that history is rarely settled, and that portraits — unlike politics — rarely lie.

A Polish Pope in Anglican England

Only in London could such a conversation begin. Seated in the Travellers Club — a place that still smells faintly of Empire and aftershave — I found myself in polite dialogue with a Roman Catholic priest. Upon discovering that I was the Polish Ambassador, he told me of his time at St George's Cathedral in Southwark and promptly invited me to deliver a lecture on Pope John Paul II. And so, on a July evening in 2023, I stood at the lectern of an English Catholic cathedral, addressing an audience about the life and legacy of a Polish pope — my compatriot, and arguably one of the most consequential figures of the twentieth century.

For a scholar of the Reformation, it was a moment heavy with irony. A Catholic pontiff, once the spiritual adversary of all things Anglican, now memorialised in a nation that broke with Rome five centuries ago. That I, a diplomat from Poland — a country that never quite severed ties with the Holy See — should be the one reflecting on this legacy in London, seemed fitting in a way neither Henry VIII nor Cardinal Wyszyński might have predicted.

John Paul II's relationship with Britain was a diplomatic achievement as much as a religious one. His 1982 visit was historic: the first by a reigning pope to set foot on British soil. That in itself was an event of remarkable symbolism in a country where papal authority had once been treated as treasonous. But there he was: a Pole in white, shaking hands with the Queen, the Supreme Governor of the Church of England.

The meeting was more than protocol. It was theatre of the most delicate kind. Behind the photographs stood centuries of doctrinal dispute, political estrangement, and cultural difference. Yet in that moment — a monarch who symbolised Anglican sovereignty and a pope who embodied Catholic universality — something resembling reconciliation took place. It was not doctrinal harmony, of course, but something quieter: mutual recognition.

That visit took place amid war. Britain was then in the middle of the Falklands conflict, and the Vatican's calls for peace were met with polite British scepticism. Still, the visit went ahead, and John Paul II managed to walk the line between pastoral concern and political tact. For all his moral certainty, he understood the value of timing.

His stop at Canterbury Cathedral was another masterstroke. There, beside the Archbishop of Canterbury, he prayed. No declarations, no dogmatic bargaining — just silence and gesture. The doctrinal chasm between Rome and Canterbury remained, of course. The ordination of women, the nature of ecclesiastical authority, the very idea of the papacy — all points of division. John Paul II did not pretend otherwise. He knew reconciliation was a long game. His genius lay in playing it.

That genius extended beyond England's shores. For the Polish diaspora in Britain, many of whom had arrived during or after the Second World War, the Pope's visit was a moment of profound pride. Their countryman — who had lived through Nazi occupation and Communist rule — now stood as moral voice on the global stage. His support for the Solidarity movement at home resonated not only in Warsaw and Gdańsk, but in the émigré communities of London, Manchester, and Edinburgh.

British political leaders recognised this, too. John Paul II's resistance to Soviet authoritarianism aligned neatly with the West's Cold War posture. Yet he was never merely an ideological ally. His insistence on human rights, his championing of religious freedom, and his critique of consumerism often placed him at odds with both sides of the ideological divide. He was not an easy friend. But he was a serious one.

There was also his interfaith work. In an age before "dialogue" became a fashionable buzzword, John Paul II practised it. His outreach to Jewish communities, his meetings with Muslim leaders, his insistence that religious identity must not become political cudgel — all of this found a receptive audience in Britain, itself grappling with questions of multiculturalism and post-colonial identity.

The paradox of John Paul II's presence in Britain lies in the fact that, though he was a conservative in doctrine, he was a pragmatist in diplomacy. He did not compromise on Catholic teaching, but he knew that gestures often precede agreement. A joint prayer with an Anglican bishop, a respectful silence in a synagogue, a handshake with an imam — these were not mere photo opportunities. They were parts of a larger theology of encounter, rooted in the belief that truth can speak without shouting.

As I spoke that day at St George's, I was struck by the quiet convergence of histories in the room. Here stood a Polish ambassador in an English cathedral, commemorating a Polish pope who had once led a global church from behind the Iron Curtain. The setting — an institution that had survived the Reformation, Blitz, and bureaucratic indifference — was a fitting stage.

Britain and Poland share more history than we often admit. Our pilots flew together in the Battle of Britain. Our soldiers bled side by side at Monte Cassino. Our political fates, so often shaped by larger powers, have nonetheless intersected with surprising frequency. John Paul II knew this. His visit acknowledged it, not with grand speeches but with gestures — a wreath here, a blessing there, a word of thanks.

That is perhaps the key to his legacy in Britain. He did not resolve our theological disputes. He did not paper over our historical wounds. But he showed that faith, when exercised with imagination and patience, can become something more than a private conviction. It can be diplomacy in cassock and mitre.

The English Reformation created deep and lasting divisions between Rome and London. But Holbein, Cromwell, More, and the others are long gone. What remains is the possibility of mutual regard. John Paul II, for all his certainty, opened space for that.

To speak of him now, in a cathedral that has witnessed centuries of change, is to remember that history does not always move by rupture. Sometimes it turns by slow degrees — through conversation, through presence, through the subtle power of showing up.

PART V

LONDON, THE STAGE OF CULTURAL ENCOUNTERS

The Warburg Institute Reborn: Memory, Scholarship, and Renewal

Dedicated to Bill Sherman, Director of the Warburg Institute, whose leadership has guided its transformation and ensured its enduring legacy.

Nearly thirty years have passed since my first research visit to the Warburg Institute, then housed in a building whose unassuming exterior belied the intellectual treasures within. I was drawn to its labyrinthine shelves, its philosophy of interdisciplinary humanism, and the indelible legacy of Aby Warburg — a man whose vision reshaped the study of cultural memory in ways that continue to inspire scholars. Now, returning not only as an academic but as a diplomat, I had the privilege of witnessing the Warburg Institute's renaissance and participating in its reopening ceremony. This revival has reaffirmed its status as a beacon of knowledge, dialogue, and scholarly inquiry.

The recently completed £14.5 million renovation, known as the "Warburg Renaissance", has ensured that the Institute remains both a sanctuary for scholars and a vital cultural institution for the wider public. Designed by the distinguished architectural firm Haworth Tompkins, the modernisation respects the Institute's historical ethos while significantly enhancing its capacity for research, education, and public engagement. The transformation embodies Warburg's spirit of inquiry, ensuring that the Institute continues to serve as a crucible for intellectual exchange.

Among the most striking additions is the Kythera Gallery, the Institute's first dedicated exhibition space. Named after one of Warburg's most evocative research subjects — Botticelli's *Birth of Venus*, which depicts the goddess arriving on the shores of Kythera — the gallery serves as a bridge between academia and the public, making the Warburg's collections more accessible than ever. The inaugural exhibition, *Memory & Migration: The Warburg Institute 1926–2024*, traced the Institute's forced relocation from Hamburg to London, drawing a poignant parallel between cultural memory and the displacement of knowledge. Another key enhancement is the Hinrich Reemtsma Auditorium, a 110-seat venue designed for lectures, film screenings, and performances. This space embodies the Warburg's enduring commitment to dialogue — not as an abstract intellectual pursuit but as a vibrant exchange of ideas. Meanwhile, the new Wohl Reading Room, bathed in natural light, invites scholars to immerse themselves in the Warburg's special collections, including rare books and manuscripts that continue to illuminate the enduring influence of classical antiquity on European thought. Perhaps most crucially, the Marie-Louise von Motesiczky Teaching Suite will allow the Warburg to engage more directly with students and young researchers. In an age when the humanities are often embattled, such investments in education affirm the continuing relevance of Warburg's interdisciplinary vision. They ensure that future generations of scholars can explore the intricate interplay of images, symbols, and texts that shape our understanding of culture.

The Warburg Institute is more than a building; it is an intellectual project that has shaped generations of scholars. Founded in Hamburg at the turn of the twentieth century, it was uprooted by the rise of National Socialism and found refuge in London, where it became part of the University of London. Central to its ethos is the "law of the good neighbour" — the principle that books should be arranged not by rigid classification but by thematic and intellectual affinities. Here, Warburg and his successors, including Fritz Saxl, Ernst Cassirer, Erwin Panofsky, and Frances Yates, pioneered a scholarly approach that dissolves disciplinary boundaries, treating art, literature, science, and philosophy as interconnected threads in the grand tapestry of human culture.

Aby Warburg's vision was revolutionary. Rejecting the purely formalist approach to art history, he sought to uncover the psychological and cultural underpinnings of imagery, tracing the survival and transformation of classical motifs across different epochs. His concept of *Nachleben der Antike* ("the afterlife of antiquity") formed the foundation for an interdisciplinary methodology that continues to shape the humanities. Warburg's ambitious *Mnemosyne Atlas*, an unfinished yet groundbreaking visual project, sought to map the migration of images and symbols across time and geography, revealing the deep structures of cultural memory.

In the early twentieth century, Warburg's collection of books and photographs grew into a private research library, and by 1926, it had evolved into a formal institute in Hamburg. However, with the rise of the Nazi regime, the Institute's existence in Germany became untenable. Thanks to the intervention of British scholars and benefactors, the entire library was relocated to London in 1933, marking the beginning of a new chapter in its history. Incorporated into the University of London in 1944, the Warburg Institute established itself as a centre for the study of intellectual and cultural history, fostering pioneering research into Renaissance thought, iconology, and the transmission of knowledge.

My introduction to the Warburg's unique methodology came in the mid-1990s, when I first encountered its seemingly chaotic yet profoundly coherent library system. As a scholar of intellectual history, I was captivated by the methodical serendipity the Warburg cultivates — one book leading to another, one idea sparking the next. The Institute was not merely a repository of knowledge but a dynamic space where ideas flourished in proximity to one another. This experience left an indelible mark on my thinking and deepened my understanding of European intellectual traditions.

Returning in 2024, I found the Warburg both transformed and reassuringly familiar. The architectural renewal has enhanced its physical spaces, yet the intellectual energy remains unchanged. The library continues to embody Warburg's principles, allowing researchers to engage in interdisciplinary exploration guided by the unexpected connections between texts and images.

As an intellectual historian, my admiration for the Warburg has only deepened over the decades. Yet as a diplomat, my recent visit took on an additional layer of significance. In 2022, I had the honour of organising a panel discussion at the Warburg Institute to commemorate the 500th anniversary of the first Polish diplomatic mission to England. Ioannes Dantiscus, the Renaissance poet and humanist who served as Poland's envoy to Henry VIII's court in 1522, epitomised the spirit of cultural exchange that the Warburg cherishes. The event, bringing together historians, scholars, and diplomats, underscored that the Warburg is not merely an academic institution but a place where history, diplomacy, and intellectual inquiry converge.

The newly renovated Warburg stands as a testament to the resilience of ideas. It has survived exile, war, and shifting intellectual fashions, emerging stronger and more vital with each challenge. At a time when the humanities face existential threats from utilitarian pressures and funding cuts, the Warburg's commitment to the longue durée of human thought is more crucial than ever. My return to the Warburg was more than a nostalgic pilgrimage. It was a reaffirmation of the values that have shaped my intellectual and diplomatic career: curiosity, dialogue, and the belief that the past continues to speak to us in unexpected ways. The Warburg Institute, with its new spaces and renewed mission, remains a place where scholars, thinkers, and visitors can engage with the great questions of cultural transmission and historical memory. It is not merely a library or an archive — it is, in the truest sense, a living institution, where the echoes of antiquity continue to inspire the present and illuminate the future.

Through the Lens: Reflections on Art Appreciation in the Digital Age

During a recent visit to the National Gallery in London, I was drawn to the much-acclaimed exhibition *Van Gogh: Poets and Lovers*. The exhibition brings together over fifty of Van Gogh's masterpieces, offering profound insight into the artist's creative process during his time in Arles and Saint-Rémy. Works such as *Starry Night over the Rhône* and *The Yellow House* stand as testaments to Van Gogh's relentless pursuit of artistic expression, his ability to render the world in swirling, pulsating strokes of colour.

As I navigated the crowded rooms, however, I was struck by a phenomenon that has become increasingly prevalent in recent years: visitors engaging with the artworks predominantly through the lenses of their smartphones. Instead of immersing themselves in the vivid colours and emotive brushstrokes that define Van Gogh's oeuvre, many were preoccupied with capturing digital replicas, perhaps to share on social media or to peruse at a later time. The very act of looking seemed secondary to the need to document.

This experience prompted a reflection on my personal journey with art and the evolving nature of its appreciation. My first encounter with the National Gallery took place in 1988, during my very first visit to Britain. As a young doctoral student from Communist Poland, I had been granted the opportunity to be a visiting scholar at St Anne's College, Oxford. Given the political climate of the time, international travel was a rare privilege, making the prospect of exploring Britain all the more thrilling. While based in Oxford, I also visited London, where I had my first opportunity to step inside the National Gallery — a moment that was both exhilarating and deeply humbling.

Prior to this visit, my exposure to Western art was largely mediated through books and reproductions. Growing up in the 1970s in the industrial city of Katowice in southern Poland, I benefited from a cultural exchange that my father, an artist and graphic designer, facilitated with counterparts abroad. He would send Polish art books to England and, in return, receive English publications. Among these treasured volumes was a guide to the National Gallery by Sir Philip Hendy, adorned with Titian's *A Man with a Quilted Sleeve* on its cover.

This book became a portal to a world beyond the Iron Curtain, igniting a fervent desire to one day stand before these masterpieces. When that aspiration materialised in 1988, I spent countless hours in the Gallery, absorbing each painting with an intensity born of years of anticipation. The tactile presence of the artworks — the texture of the paint, the subtle nuances of colour, the scale — offered an experience that no reproduction could replicate. This direct engagement fostered a deep, personal connection with the art, each piece revealing its secrets through prolonged contemplation.

In subsequent years, during research visits to the Warburg Institute and as a tourist, I returned to the National Gallery numerous times. Each visit reaffirmed the Gallery as a sanctuary, a space where art could be encountered in its purest form, unmarred by external distractions. The act of looking — truly looking — became a meditative practice, a dialogue between the viewer and the artwork.

Contrasting these experiences with the present trend of viewing art through smartphone cameras is, for me, disconcerting. The proliferation of digital devices has undoubtedly democratised access to art, allowing individuals to capture and share their experiences instantaneously. However, this convenience may come at the cost of genuine engagement. The lens, while capturing the image, can also serve as a barrier, distancing the viewer from the immediate, visceral experience of the artwork.

Art galleries are, in essence, sanctuaries — spaces designed to facilitate a direct encounter with creativity, emotion, and history. They invite us to pause, to reflect, to immerse ourselves in the artist's vision. When this engagement is mediated through a screen, we risk reducing the artwork to a mere visual commodity, stripped of its depth and resonance.

This shift in art appreciation reflects broader societal changes. The digital age has ushered in an era of immediacy, where experiences are often curated for online consumption, sometimes at the expense of personal reflection. The compulsion to document and share can overshadow the act of experiencing itself.

Yet, there is hope in the enduring allure of art. The very presence of crowds at exhibitions like *Van Gogh: Poets and Lovers* attests to a collective yearning for beauty, for connection, for meaning. Perhaps the challenge lies in recalibrating our approach, in recognising the value of unmediated engagement.

In this context, the method of Professor Jennifer Roberts, an art historian at Harvard University, offers a compelling counterpoint. She requires her students to select a painting and spend three uninterrupted hours observing it, noting their evolving observations and questions. This exercise in "slow looking" encourages deep engagement, allowing viewers to uncover details and insights that a cursory glance would miss. Roberts argues that such patience and immersive attention are essential skills, particularly in an age dominated by rapid information consumption.

As I stood before *Sunflowers*, I consciously put away my smartphone. I allowed myself to be enveloped by the vibrant yellows, the dynamic brushstrokes, the palpable energy that Van Gogh infused into the canvas. In that moment, I was reminded of the profound impact that direct observation can have — a reminder of why art matters, and why our manner of engaging with it is of equal importance.

While technology offers unprecedented access to art, it is imperative that we remain mindful of how we engage with these cultural treasures. Let us not allow the convenience of digital devices to eclipse the rich, rewarding experience of direct observation. For it is through our eyes, unmediated and attentive, that we truly connect with the soul of the artwork and, by extension, with the humanity it embodies.

The Magic of London's Bookshops

Few cities in the world allow one to step into a bookshop and feel instantly at home, regardless of origin. London is one such city. Its bookshops are not merely repositories of printed words but sanctuaries, cultural landmarks, and quiet bastions of resistance against an increasingly digital world. As a foreign ambassador in London, I have come to appreciate these literary havens in ways I had not anticipated. They offer not only literary treasures but also a window into the very soul of the city.

Among London's many bookshops, Daunt Books in Marylebone remains my favourite. There is something deeply reassuring about its Edwardian oak galleries, the scent of paper that greets visitors upon entry, and the quiet murmur of customers engrossed in their own worlds. While Daunt is best known for its travel section, arranged geographically rather than by genre, what draws me most is its exceptional collection of books on Poland. It is heartening to see a London bookshop curating a section dedicated to my homeland, offering both canonical works and lesser-known gems. On many occasions, I have found myself recommending titles to curious readers seeking to understand Poland beyond the headlines. In these moments, books become diplomatic instruments, fostering cultural connections that formal meetings rarely achieve.

London's bookshops each possess a distinct character, shaped by their location, selection, and patrons. Hatchards, on Piccadilly, is the grandest of them all. Established in 1797, it exudes an air of quiet tradition. Its shelves have been perused by prime ministers, novelists, and monarchs alike. Here, literature and history intersect, making it nearly impossible to leave without acquiring a volume or two. In its carefully curated displays, I have discovered first editions of Polish authors, unexpected translations, and political memoirs that have deepened my understanding of both Britain and my own country.

If Hatchards represents the grandeur of British literary tradition, then Foyles on Charing Cross Road embodies its modern evolution. A labyrinth of floors filled with an astonishing array of titles, Foyles is a paradise for anyone who enjoys getting lost among books. The intellectual energy of London is palpable here, where students pore over philosophy texts and novelists scribble notes in the café. What makes Foyles particularly appealing to me is its international selection, reflecting London's status as a global capital. Here, I have found Polish books that had eluded me even in Warsaw. In such moments, London feels smaller, more intimately connected to my roots, as though the city itself understands the need to carry fragments of home across borders.

For those seeking something beyond the mainstream, London offers bookshops that feel like hidden treasures, each with its own niche and particular charm. Lutyens & Rubinstein in Notting Hill is one such place — a haven for serious readers who appreciate beautifully bound editions and expert recommendations. The staff possess an encyclopaedic knowledge of literature, and I often leave with books I had not intended to buy but suddenly cannot wait to read. Likewise, Persephone Books, though recently relocated, remains a unique part of London's literary landscape. Specialising in forgotten works by women writers, it is a bookshop that revives voices history might otherwise have silenced. As someone who has spent much of my career immersed in literature, I find Persephone's mission particularly admirable.

For those with a taste for the esoteric, the antiquarian bookshops of Cecil Court are an irresistible draw. Walking down this narrow passageway feels like stepping back in time, with shopfronts displaying rare books, maps, and prints. Some of these establishments have been selling books for over a century, their interiors resembling private libraries from another era. Here, I have found rare editions of Polish poetry, historical accounts of Britain's relations with Poland, and unexpected curiosities that remind me how deeply intertwined our histories have been. These bookshops are not merely places to acquire books; they are living archives, custodians of literary and historical memory.

No exploration of London's bookshops would be complete without mentioning the Polish Bookshop at POSK in Hammersmith. Serving as both a cultural hub and a testament to London's long-standing Polish presence, it has provided generations of Polish immigrants and visitors with a connection to their heritage. Here, one can find Polish fiction, poetry, historical studies, and even the latest releases from Warsaw publishing houses. It is more than a bookshop; it is a meeting place, a bridge between the Polish community and the broader literary landscape of London. Whenever I visit, I am reminded of the resilience of Polish culture and its ability to thrive even in exile. The bookshop's shelves tell a story of survival, adaptation, and the enduring power of literature to sustain identity.

London's bookshops are more than places of commerce; they are spaces of discovery, dialogue, and quiet contemplation. In each of them, I have encountered a different facet of the city's character — its tradition and innovation, its openness to the world, and its reverence for the written word. As a diplomat, I often reflect on the formal mechanisms of cultural exchange — the summits and discussions that shape international relations. Yet, in truth, much of that work happens in quieter ways: through the books we read, the conversations they spark, and the shared understanding they foster.

Whenever I step into a London bookshop, I am reminded of why I fell in love with books in the first place. They are portals to other worlds, yet they also serve as anchors to the past. In a foreign city, they offer familiarity and surprise in equal measure. And in an increasingly fragmented world, they remain among the few places where we can still find common ground, one page at a time.

A Tale of Two Collections: Polish Treasures in New York and London

Among the myriad museums I've had the pleasure of visiting, two stand out for their intimate charm and exceptional collections: The Frick Collection in New York and the Wallace Collection in London. Both institutions, though modest in scale compared to sprawling national museums, offer a curated experience that allows visitors to engage deeply with art and history. Notably, each houses significant pieces connected to Polish heritage, adding a personal resonance to their galleries.

The Frick Collection, nestled in the heart of Manhattan, is renowned for its assemblage of European masterpieces. Among its treasures is Rembrandt's enigmatic painting *The Polish Rider*. Created around 1655, this artwork depicts a young man astride a horse, traversing a mysterious landscape. The rider's attire — a fur-lined cap and a long riding coat — bears a striking resemblance to the traditional dress of Polish light cavalry officers of the seventeenth century. This connection has led scholars to speculate on the subject's identity, with some suggesting he represents a Polish noble or soldier.

The painting's journey to The Frick Collection is as intriguing as its subject. It was once part of the collection of King Stanisław II August Poniatowski of Poland, who referred to it as the *Cossack on Horseback*. In the early twentieth century, it was acquired by Henry Clay Frick, finding a permanent home in New York. The painting's presence in The Frick Collection serves as a testament to the enduring cultural exchanges between Poland and the wider world.

Across the Atlantic, nestled in London's Manchester Square, the Wallace Collection offers an exquisite array of fine and decorative arts. Among its holdings are significant Polish artefacts, notably a seventeenth-century Polish hussar's armour and several Polish sabres. The Polish hussars, often referred to as "winged hussars", were an elite cavalry unit famed for their distinctive armour adorned with wing-like structures. This armour not only provided protection but also symbolised the hussars' formidable presence on the battlefield. The Wallace Collection's display of such armour offers visitors a tangible link to Poland's rich military history.

Similarly, the collection's Polish sabres exemplify the craftsmanship and martial traditions of Poland. These curved swords, known for their elegance and effectiveness in combat, are emblematic of the Polish cavalry's prowess. Their inclusion in the Wallace Collection underscores the museum's dedication to representing diverse cultural artefacts.

Both The Frick Collection and the Wallace Collection share striking similarities. Housed in historic mansions, they offer an intimate viewing experience, allowing visitors to engage closely with the artworks. Their founders, Henry Clay Frick and Sir Richard Wallace, were discerning collectors who favoured quality over quantity, resulting in collections that are both cohesive and comprehensive.

The presence of Polish artefacts in these museums highlights the global appreciation and recognition of Poland's cultural and historical contributions. Rembrandt's *The Polish Rider* in New York and the hussar's armour and sabres in London serve as cultural ambassadors, fostering a deeper understanding of Poland's artistic and martial heritage.

The allure of museums like The Frick Collection and the Wallace Collection lies in their manageable scale and the personal nature of their exhibits. Unlike larger institutions, where one might feel overwhelmed by the sheer volume of displays, these museums provide a serene environment conducive to contemplation and appreciation.

Visitors can leisurely explore the galleries, each room thoughtfully arranged to showcase the artworks in harmonious contexts. This intimate setting allows for a more profound connection with the pieces, enabling one to appreciate the nuances and stories each object holds.

In a world where cultural institutions often vie for grandeur and scale, The Frick Collection and the Wallace Collection stand as reminders of the beauty found in thoughtful curation and intimate settings. Their dedication to preserving and showcasing artefacts of global significance, including those from Poland, offers visitors an enriching experience that transcends borders and time.

As I reflect on these museums, I am reminded of the words of the Polish poet Wisława Szymborska: "We are extremely fortunate not to know precisely the kind of world we live in." In the halls of The Frick Collection and the Wallace Collection, we are invited to explore this unknown, to discover connections, and to find joy in the shared heritage of humanity.

Felix Fabian and Lili Stern-Pohlmann: A Legacy of Art and Resilience

The annals of twentieth-century history are replete with extraordinary lives shaped by the dual forces of creative brilliance and historical upheaval. Among these stand Felix Fabian, a painter and multi-talented artist, and Lili Stern-Pohlmann, a Holocaust survivor and cultural advocate. Their intertwined lives reveal not only the enduring power of art but also the resilience of the human spirit. Through Fabian's paintings and Stern-Pohlmann's steadfast dedication to preserving his legacy, we are offered a poignant testament to the redemptive capacities of creativity and memory.

Felix Fabian's story begins in Warsaw, a city pulsating with artistic and intellectual fervour before the Second World War. Born into a Jewish family, Fabian displayed an early aptitude for art, which led him to study in Warsaw, Vienna, and Rome. This European education endowed him with a cosmopolitan sensibility that would characterise his later works. However, the trajectory of Fabian's life, like that of many of his contemporaries, was irrevocably altered by the outbreak of war.

As war engulfed Europe, Fabian found himself swept into its maelstrom. His escape to the Soviet Union and eventual enlistment in the Polish Army in exile became the foundation of a journey that spanned continents. Amidst the harrowing realities of wartime, Fabian's creativity flourished in unexpected ways. Serving in a theatrical troupe attached to the Polish Army, he painted, acted, and designed sets, using his artistic skills to uplift the morale of soldiers. His watercolours from this period, such as *Advancing Soldiers* (1942), capture the resilience and camaraderie of wartime life, illustrating his capacity to find beauty amidst adversity.

Following the war, Fabian's peripatetic life continued, taking him to Italy, where he worked with the famed Cinecittà film studios, and eventually to London and Buenos Aires. In these cosmopolitan centres, Fabian's art gained recognition. He painted portraits of luminaries such as Winston Churchill and Pope Pius XII and explored themes that reflected his own complex identity, including scenes of Jewish life and culture. His ability to adapt his medium and style to different contexts underscores his versatility as an artist. Yet, Fabian remained a figure largely unrecognised by the wider art world — his work a hidden gem waiting to be rediscovered.

Enter Lili Stern-Pohlmann, a figure as remarkable as Fabian himself. Born in Lwów (modern-day Lviv) in 1930, Stern-Pohlmann's early life was marked by unimaginable loss and courage. Her father and younger brother were killed during the Holocaust, while she and her mother survived thanks to the bravery of individuals such as Irmgard Wieth, a German civil servant, and Archbishop Andrei Sheptytsky, who sheltered them in a convent. These experiences instilled in Stern-Pohlmann a profound commitment to fostering understanding between cultures and preserving the memory of those who perished.

Stern-Pohlmann's path crossed with Fabian's in London, where she became one of his staunchest supporters and closest confidantes. Their friendship blossomed in the vibrant milieu of London's post-war émigré community, a gathering place for displaced artists, intellectuals, and visionaries. Stern-Pohlmann's home became a repository for Fabian's art, as she meticulously collected and preserved his paintings, drawings, and sketches. Her efforts ensured that Fabian's legacy would not be relegated to obscurity but instead celebrated as a vital part of Polish-Jewish and European cultural heritage.

The relationship between Fabian and Stern-Pohlmann was not merely one of artist and patron but of mutual inspiration.

Fabian's portraits of Stern-Pohlmann — imbued with sensitivity and nuance — reflect her role as both muse and moral compass. In turn, Stern-Pohlmann saw in Fabian's art a powerful medium for storytelling and cultural bridge-building. Her commitment to his work extended beyond mere preservation; she sought to contextualise his oeuvre within the broader narratives of displacement, identity, and resilience that defined their generation.

In February 2025, this shared legacy was brought to light in a landmark exhibition at POSK, the Polish Social and Cultural Association in Hammersmith, London. The exhibition, *Paintings by Felix Fabian from the Collection of Lili Stern-Pohlmann*, opened on 1 February and offered a rare glimpse into Fabian's artistic journey, encompassing everything from his delicate watercolours to his bold oil portraits. It also highlighted Stern-Pohlmann's tireless efforts to ensure that his work reaches contemporary audiences. Through this collection, visitors were invited to reflect on the ways in which art serves as both a personal expression and a communal memory, bridging past and present.

A particularly momentous occasion took place on 5 February 2025, when His Majesty King Charles III visited POSK and toured the exhibition. The exhibition showcased Fabian's evocative depictions of his home in Poland and his subsequent travels. His works followed the combat route of the Polish Second Corps in the Middle East and Italy, before his post-war emigration to Argentina and eventual settlement in London. The paintings, from the rich collection of the late Lili Stern-Pohlmann, offered a compelling visual narrative of displacement, resilience, and artistic mastery. The King's visit underscored the cultural significance of Fabian's work and the invaluable contributions of the Polish community in Britain.

Fabian's artistic versatility was one of the exhibition's central revelations. His portraits, whether of Stern-Pohlmann or international figures, exude a striking immediacy, capturing not only physical likenesses but also the intangible essence of his subjects. His Jewish-themed works, inspired by his reconnection with his heritage through Stern-Pohlmann, are equally compelling. Pieces like *Shabbat Shalom* (1967) convey a profound sense of cultural pride and continuity, juxtaposing the vibrancy of Jewish traditions with the artist's own diasporic experience.

The exhibition also shed light on Stern-Pohlmann's extraordinary life and contributions. Beyond her role as a collector, she was an advocate for Holocaust education and Polish-Jewish dialogue, earning accolades such as the Order of the British Empire. Her life encapsulates the dual imperatives of remembrance and action, reminding us that the preservation of history is not a passive act but an active engagement with its lessons. Stern-Pohlmann's decision to share Fabian's work with the public reflected her belief in art's capacity to foster empathy and understanding — a belief as vital today as it was in her time.

At its core, the story of Felix Fabian and Lili Stern-Pohlmann is a story of resilience. Both individuals, in their own ways, transcended the traumas of displacement and war, channelling their experiences into creative and cultural achievements. Their legacy challenges us to consider the ways in which art serves as a form of resistance, a means of preserving identity, and a bridge between seemingly disparate worlds.

In an age marked by polarisation and cultural amnesia, the example set by Fabian and Stern-Pohlmann is profoundly instructive. Fabian's art, with its universal themes of humanity and perseverance, invites us to look beyond borders and labels, while Stern-Pohlmann's advocacy reminds us of our shared responsibility to remember and learn from history. Together, they exemplify the enduring relevance of art and memory as tools for dialogue and connection.

As we admire Fabian's paintings and reflect on Stern-Pohlmann's life, we are reminded that the preservation of culture is not merely an academic exercise but a deeply human endeavour. Through such efforts, the legacies of individuals like Fabian and Stern-Pohlmann continue to inspire, offering a vision of a world in which art and empathy prevail over division and forgetfulness.

Wigmore Hall: A Sanctuary
of Music in London

Nestled in the heart of London's West End, Wigmore Hall stands as one of the city's most treasured cultural institutions. It is a place where the intimacy of chamber music finds its ideal setting, where voices resonate with crystalline clarity, and where generations of audiences have discovered the profound beauty of live performance. For me, this hall has been more than just a venue; it has been a sanctuary, a source of inspiration, and a space where music transcends the everyday and reaches into the sublime.

My personal journey with Wigmore Hall began in the early 1990s when I arrived in London as a visiting postgraduate scholar. Like many before me, I was drawn to the city's grandeur, its layers of history, and its inexhaustible cultural offerings. It was during one of my exploratory walks through Marylebone that I first noticed the elegant, understated façade of Wigmore Hall. Curiosity led me inside, and from the moment I took my seat in the intimate auditorium, I knew I had stumbled upon something extraordinary.

Wigmore Hall was built in 1901 as Bechstein Hall, commissioned by the German piano manufacturer C. Bechstein Pianofortefabrik. Designed by the British architect Thomas Edward Collcutt, the hall exudes a restrained elegance, with its alabaster and marble interior culminating in an exquisite domed ceiling. This dome, adorned with a mural by Gerald Moira depicting *The Soul of Music*, imbues the space with an ethereal glow, making the hall not only a listening experience but a visual one as well. Its acoustics, revered by musicians and audiences alike, are among the finest in Europe, allowing the subtlest nuances of a performance to be heard with perfect clarity.

Over the decades, Wigmore Hall has become synonymous with chamber music and art song, hosting some of the greatest musicians of the twentieth and twenty-first centuries. Sergey Prokofiev, Benjamin Britten, Francis Poulenc — all have performed here, adding to its illustrious history. The pianist Alfred Brendel once remarked, "For chamber music and song, there is no hall in the world that has better acoustics than Wigmore Hall." Such sentiments echo through generations of performers who have graced its stage, each leaving an indelible mark on its musical legacy.

One of the hall's most remarkable aspects is its ability to bridge generations, presenting both legends of the classical world and emerging talents. In recent years, I have been particularly gratified to witness the presence of exceptional Polish artists on its stage. The countertenor Jakub Józef Orliński, whose voice possesses a rare and haunting beauty, has captivated audiences here with his unique blend of technical mastery and emotional depth. Pianist Aleksandra Mysłek, whose performances exhibit both sensitivity and precision, has also made her mark in this hallowed space. The Silesian String Quartet, one of Poland's most respected chamber ensembles, has brought the richness of Polish classical tradition to Wigmore Hall's audiences, performing works by Lutosławski, Maliszewski, and Weinberg. Seeing Polish artists perform in this historic setting reinforces the deep cultural ties between Poland and the United Kingdom, a relationship that extends beyond politics and diplomacy into the realm of shared artistic appreciation.

One of Wigmore Hall's defining characteristics is its unwavering dedication to excellence. Unlike larger concert venues, which often cater to a broad spectrum of musical tastes, Wigmore Hall remains steadfast in its mission to present chamber music and song recitals at the highest level. This is reflected not only in the calibre of its performers but also in its carefully curated programmes, which frequently feature lesser-known masterpieces alongside canonical works. The hall has also been a champion of contemporary music, commissioning new works that push the boundaries of the classical tradition while remaining true to its spirit.

Beyond its musical offerings, Wigmore Hall possesses an atmosphere unlike any other concert venue in London. There is an intimacy here that fosters a rare connection between performer and audience. In the hush before a recital begins, one feels a collective sense of anticipation, a shared reverence for the music about to unfold. The absence of amplified sound creates an experience that is both immediate and immersive, where every breath of the performer, every articulation of a phrase, is deeply felt. I still recall an evening when an encore performance of Schubert's *Ständchen* held the audience in complete silence, the final note lingering in the air as if suspended in time. The sheer magic of such moments is what makes Wigmore Hall incomparable.

Wigmore Hall has long been a place of inspiration not only for musicians but also for writers. Though it does not feature prominently in literature in the way that, say, Covent Garden or the Royal Opera House does, its presence can be found in the memoirs and letters of many musicians and music lovers who have passed through its doors. The composer Ralph Vaughan Williams, who performed here frequently, once described it as "a musician's hall, where the music itself is the star". It is a space that invites reflection, where the experience of music is heightened by the hall's historic grandeur. One imagines the great figures of the past — composers, critics, enthusiasts — sitting in these same seats, enraptured by the performances unfolding before them.

My connection to Wigmore Hall has deepened over the years, from my early days as a student to my current role as Poland's ambassador to the United Kingdom. Amid the responsibilities of diplomacy, I have often sought refuge here, finding solace in the universal language of music. Each visit reaffirms my belief in the power of culture to transcend borders, to foster understanding, and to remind us of our shared humanity.

Wigmore Hall is not merely a concert venue; it is a living testament to the enduring power of music. It stands as a reminder that in an age of rapid technological advancement, where attention is increasingly fragmented, there remains an appetite for deep, meaningful artistic experiences. It is a place where time slows, where one can step away from the demands of daily life and enter a world of sonic beauty. As Alfred Brendel once said, "To play at Wigmore Hall is to engage in a dialogue with history." For me, and for countless others, it remains a sanctuary — a space where music speaks directly to the soul.

Auberon Herbert: The Forgotten Friend of Poland and Eastern Europe

To Jan Chodakowski, from whom I first learned about Herbert.

Auberon Mark Herbert is hardly a household name, even among historians of Britain's twentieth-century foreign relations. Yet his life embodies a romantic and paradoxical devotion to Eastern Europe that is unmatched in his generation. Born into the British aristocracy — his father, Colonel Aubrey Herbert, a Conservative MP and war hero — Auberon defied every expectation of his class. Rather than seek comfort or prestige, he dedicated his life to the struggles of others, particularly the displaced and forgotten nations of Central and Eastern Europe. When he died unexpectedly in 1974 at Pixton Park, the family home in Somerset, his passing was largely overlooked in Britain. But within the scattered communities of Polish, Belarusian, Ukrainian, and Hungarian émigrés, Herbert's death was mourned as the loss of a compatriot. He was, in every meaningful sense, a man who chose his own country — and it was not his own.

Denied entry into the British Army on medical grounds, Herbert refused to remain on the sidelines of war. After failed attempts to join the Free French and Dutch forces, he turned to the Polish Armed Forces in exile. Enlisting in 1940, he was eventually commissioned as a second lieutenant and fought alongside General Stanisław Maczek's 1st Polish Armoured Division in the campaign through Normandy and the Low Countries. His loyalty was no mere token of solidarity. Captured in Ghent by Canadian military police who suspected him of espionage, Herbert suffered a beating so severe that it left permanent scars. His appearance, accent, and polyglot speech had led to a cruel irony: the British aristocrat mistaken for a spy while serving under a foreign flag. Yet he wore his Polish uniform with evident pride, forming bonds that would shape the rest of his life.

When peace came to Western Europe, Herbert did not retreat from the struggles he had embraced. With the Iron Curtain descending, he turned his energies to those left stateless, voiceless, and dispossessed by the new order. His advocacy extended far beyond Poland. In time, he became a benefactor and champion of Belarusians, Ukrainians, and Hungarians, opening his home, his wallet, and his reputation in their defence. For many displaced persons, Herbert was a godsend. He helped resettle Polish soldiers and their families, even financing a textile factory to provide jobs. He supported underground publications and lent his influence to initiatives that kept alive the memory and identity of occupied nations. In 1954, he co-founded the Anglo-Belarusian Society, serving as its chairman for the rest of his life.

Herbert never viewed his support as mere charity. He did not simply help the East European émigrés; he lived among them. Fluent in multiple languages, including Polish, he moved seamlessly between aristocratic drawing rooms and the more modest quarters of displaced intellectuals, former soldiers, and clergy. He was the rare kind of aristocrat who used his title not for personal gain but to lend weight to others' causes. If his name opened doors, it was always others he ushered through. He never demanded centre stage, but he was always at the heart of the story. His villa in Portofino and the family estate at Pixton became informal embassies of lost nations — places where memory, resistance, and hope could endure.

His spiritual life was no less entwined with the cause of the exiles. A committed Catholic, Herbert became disillusioned with the reforms of the Second Vatican Council. He sought out instead the ancient liturgies of the Eastern Church. At the Belarusian Catholic Church in Finchley, he found both a form of worship and a fellowship of spirit. That church, with its

Byzantine-Slavonic rite, became his spiritual home. In faith as in friendship, Herbert identified with those whose traditions had been suppressed. When he died at the age of fifty-two, it was Belarusian Catholic clergy who conducted his funeral — not in a grand aristocratic spectacle, but in a quiet, deeply personal ceremony.

There were, inevitably, whispers of intelligence connections. His name appears in a declassified American document as one of two British Conservatives who met with the exiled Ukrainian nationalist Yaroslav Stetsko in 1951. Some have suggested he may have acted as an informal conduit for British interests during the early Cold War, though definitive proof remains elusive. Herbert himself made no claim to espionage, and he would likely have dismissed such speculation. What cannot be denied is that he moved freely within exile circles that were often under surveillance, and that his activities often aligned with Britain's quiet opposition to Soviet expansionism. Whether as an informal operative or simply an eccentric Englishman with an unbending moral compass, he became a thorn in the side of the regimes behind the Iron Curtain. His exclusion from Poland in the 1960s was likely inevitable.

And yet, for all his impact, Herbert remains a curiously under-recognised figure. His life does not feature in grand narratives of the Cold War or in official memorials. There are no statues, no state honours. Perhaps that is fitting. He lived not for public acclaim but for private conviction. He did not speak of duty, but of friendship. His legacy lies in the stories of those he helped: the soldier resettled, the dissident published, the culture preserved. He reminds us that diplomacy is not solely the work of embassies and ministers. Sometimes it is the work of one man, standing between his world and another, refusing to look away.

One wonders what Herbert would make of Eastern Europe today. Would he recognise the old dilemmas in the war in

Ukraine, in the repression of Belarus, in the fragile balancing of Poland within a contested Europe? Almost certainly he would. He would be there, writing letters, offering his home, quietly supporting those without a country. His belief in national dignity, spiritual belonging, and the obligations of conscience would not have wavered.

To remember Auberon Herbert is to remember that the bonds between nations are forged not only in treaties but in lives. His was a life of quiet heroism, of moral courage, of unstinting loyalty to people not his own. In an age that too often forgets such virtues, his example remains not only relevant but urgent.

The Quiet Witness: Adam Czerniawski and the Power of Translation

From war-torn Warsaw to the gentle hills of Wales, the life of Adam Czerniawski traced an arc emblematic of Europe's tumultuous twentieth century. Born in 1934 into a well-to-do Warsaw family, he was only a boy when the Second World War cast him into exile. In 1941 his family escaped occupied Poland via Istanbul to the Middle East, finding refuge in Turkey, Lebanon, and the British Mandate of Palestine. There the young Czerniawski attended Polish-run schools in Jerusalem and Beirut, coming of age amid a polyglot diaspora. He absorbed Hebrew and Arabic alongside his native Polish, an early immersion in cultural diversity that would later underpin his role as a bridge between nations. By the time he arrived in England in 1947, a thirteen-year-old refugee, his world had been irrevocably shaped by displacement — a formative *Wanderjahr* that endowed him with lifelong perspective and resilience. Yet if his childhood was upended, it also instilled in him a profound appreciation for the continuity of culture. In Britain he would dedicate himself to that continuity, emerging over the decades as a major literary figure in both Polish and English contexts.

Czerniawski's intellectual formation in his adopted country was distinguished. He read English literature and philosophy at the University of London and furthered his studies at Oxford and Sussex, gaining a deep grounding in the Western canon to complement his Polish heritage. This dual education — in the Romantic poetry of his homeland and the humanist traditions of England — gave Czerniawski an unusually broad cultural fluency. By his mid-twenties he was writing and publishing in Polish, even as he moved with ease in English literary circles. He became a stalwart of the post-war Polish émigré intelligentsia, yet remained very much at home in British academia and letters.

This rare double allegiance would define his career. To Poles, he was one of their own: a poet and essayist carrying forward Poland's literary patrimony abroad. To Britons, he became known above all as the eloquent translator who unlocked that patrimony for English readers.

In the 1950s and '60s, Czerniawski threw himself into the vibrant literary life of the Polish diaspora. He contributed to *Wiadomości* (the London-based émigré review) and to the Paris journal *Kultura*, two flagship platforms of free Polish thought during the Cold War. Still in his mid-twenties, he co-founded in 1959 a new magazine in London called *Kontynenty* ("Continents"). As its editor-in-chief, Czerniawski gave voice to a younger generation of Polish exiles determined to sustain a lively, unshackled intellectual culture abroad. *Kontynenty* — true to its name — spanned the horizons, welcoming writers from across continents and challenging the orthodoxies of older émigré circles. Though the magazine ran only a few years, it made a mark as a *forum liberum* for Polish literary talent unbound by faction. These editorial endeavours established Czerniawski as a discerning critic and cultural facilitator. He was keenly aware that literature in exile must serve as both a link to the past and a beacon to the future. In later years, as Poland's political climate thawed, he would also publish in the homeland's journals and presses, helping to reconnect the two sundered halves of Polish literary life.

Alongside his work as an editor and critic, Adam Czerniawski developed his own voice as a poet of considerable depth. He began publishing poetry as early as 1955, and over the next few decades his verse appeared in Polish-language volumes issued variously in London, Paris, and Kraków. Polish critics came to label him a "poet of culture", and with good reason. His poetry is richly allusive, drawing on classical motifs and European art to grapple with the existential questions of his age. A poem of his might invoke Vermeer's serene painting *View of Delft* or an ancient myth, yet always with an undercurrent of personal reflection and philosophical insight. The aesthetic surface of his work often conceals, or gently reveals, the deeper imprint of history on his psyche. For Czerniawski never forgot the ruptures of his own early life: the before and after of war and exile. There is a measured melancholy in some of his later poems, a sense of irretrievable loss — what he once referred to as an "annihilated childhood" buried in the diasporic past. But if sorrow was an undertone, it was balanced by erudition and irony. He possessed a rare ability to contemplate human suffering through the stabilising lens of art and intellect. In his lyrical universe, high culture and harsh memory converse, yielding poems of quietly intense feeling and meditative grace. It is a poetry at once steeped in tradition and unmistakably shaped by the disturbances of modern history.

Czerniawski's reputation, however, rests not only on his original writings but equally on his extraordinary achievements as a translator. He was, in effect, a one-man cultural embassy, conveying the riches of Polish literature to the Anglophone world with precision and passion. Over the years he translated hundreds of poems spanning five centuries of Polish verse — from the Renaissance psalms and epigrams of Jan Kochanowski to the stark, minimalist lines of Tadeusz Różewicz and the visionary irony of Cyprian Norwid. These were no facile exercises in dictionary equivalence. Czerniawski approached translation as a creative art, striving to recreate in English the vitality and nuance that made the Polish originals endure. Kochanowski's *Laments*, for example, he rendered with a balance of eloquence and earthiness that retained their human warmth; Różewicz's modernist fragments he delivered in austere, honed English that mirrored their spare power. Thanks to Czerniawski's effort, English readers could, perhaps for the first time, truly hear the voice of a Kochanowski or a Różewicz as something immediate and alive, rather than distant echoes from a foreign tongue. Beyond poetry, he also translated Polish prose, drama, and works of philosophy — from the aphoristic plays of Zbigniew Herbert to essays by Leszek Kołakowski — always guided by the same rigorous fidelity to meaning and tone. It is no exaggeration to say that Adam Czerniawski was a principal conduit through which post-war Britain came to discover the breadth of Polish letters. Indeed, his translation of Różewicz's poems earned him a British Arts Council award in 1976, and he was long regarded as the preeminent interpreter of that poet in English. Such honours, alongside a prestigious Polish literary prize he received in 1971, underscored how he had come to be held in equal esteem on both sides of Europe.

In Britain, Czerniawski combined his literary pursuits with an active academic and public life. He lectured on philosophy at Thames Polytechnic in London and taught literature and aesthetics at the Medway College of Design in Rochester, sharing with students his expansive humanistic outlook. For a time he even scripted cultural programmes for the BBC's Polish-language broadcasts, further spreading knowledge of Poland's heritage. In the 1980s and '90s, as scholarly interest in translation grew, Czerniawski played an integral role at the British Centre for Literary Translation at the University of East Anglia. There he mentored aspiring translators, imparting both the techniques and the ethos of literary translation — an ethos he exemplified through his own work, stressing that sincerity and exactitude are the twin pillars of any cross-cultural dialogue. His colleagues and students remember him as a man of unassuming sincerity and formidable rigour. Soft-spoken and modest, he nevertheless held the highest standards for himself and others, never indulging in easy praise or compromising on intellectual honesty. He had a way of instilling in those around him a sense that to engage with literature was a serious, almost sacred calling — one that demanded devotion, but which in return offered the profound reward of shared understanding across cultures.

Despite his vast contributions, Czerniawski never sought the limelight. He remained at heart a gentle custodian of culture, content to let the works speak louder than the worker. In an era when many intellectuals were swept up by ideological fashions, he kept a principled distance from partisan feuds. His loyalty was to literature itself — to the Polish poetic tradition he loved and to the English language that had welcomed him. That quiet integrity earned him admiration in literary circles from Warsaw to London. Over time, as Poland regained its freedom and its émigré sons and daughters were written back into national memory, Czerniawski was recognised as an important figure in Polish letters. Volumes of his collected poems and essays were published in his native country, and he occasionally returned there as a guest lecturer and mentor to the post-1989 generation. Yet it was in Britain that he spent most of his life, in a self-chosen exile that became a fruitful home. In his later years he settled in the historic Welsh town of Monmouth, where he continued to write and reflect in tranquillity.

It was in Monmouth, early in 2024, that Adam Czerniawski's long journey finally came to rest. At his funeral in the local church, family members and friends from both Britain and Poland gathered to honour a life lived in the service of letters. The ceremony was, by all accounts, simple and dignified — qualities that mirrored the man himself. There was a sense, as eulogies recounted his achievements, that Czerniawski embodied a disappearing breed: a scholar-poet of the old European tradition, multilingual, steeped in history, driven not by fame but by fidelity to his craft. There was sorrow at his passing, but also deep gratitude for the legacy he leaves behind. That legacy is evident in the countless readers who have discovered Polish literature through his translations, in the poets and translators he inspired, and in the very idea of cultural conversation that he championed. Adam Czerniawski's life reminds us that the barricades of language and nation can be crossed with empathy and intellect. In a detached, thoughtful manner he devoted decades to bridging the gap between Poland and the West, between past and present — and in doing so he became a bridge himself. Now, even as we reflect on the end of his remarkable story, the words he translated and the words he wrote continue to resonate, carrying forward his voice. It is a quiet voice, but clear and enduring, testifying that art and truth outlast the tumult of history.

A Taste of Poland in London: History, Culture, and Cuisine

London, a city where one can dine on everything from Michelin-starred foam to a kebab consumed in regret at 3 a.m., also harbours a hidden culinary treasure: Polish cuisine. As Poland's Ambassador to the United Kingdom, I may be slightly biased, but allow me to argue that Polish restaurants in London offer not only comfort and sustenance but also an invitation to experience a piece of history, an echo of exile, and — if you order the vodka flights — a mild headache the next morning.

No discussion of Polish dining in London can begin without mentioning Daquise. Located in South Kensington, this venerable establishment has been serving *pierogi* and intrigue since 1947. It is a place steeped in history, a canteen for Polish émigrés, a haunt of spies, and, according to some, a site of Cold War secrets swapped over a bowl of *barszcz*. Christine Keeler, of Profumo Affair fame, was known to frequent it, and one cannot help but wonder if the waiters have heard more state secrets than some Whitehall mandarins. Walking into Daquise is akin to stepping into another era. The wood-panelled interior, the crisp white tablecloths, the air of quiet sophistication — all suggest that here, meals are serious affairs, and so are the conversations that accompany them.

Contrast this with Ognisko Polskie, the Polish Hearth Club, another South Kensington landmark but one with a distinctly different atmosphere. Established in 1940 as a home away from home for Polish officers stranded in Britain after the fall of France, it has evolved into something more than a restaurant — it is an institution. It is where Polish London gathers to celebrate, to reminisce, to commiserate, and, on occasion, to attempt Polish folk dancing after one too many *nalewkas*. The building itself is a magnificent Victorian edifice, grand and imposing, yet

145

the restaurant inside is warm and inviting, offering a menu that bridges the gap between tradition and modernity.

The key difference between Daquise and Ognisko? At Daquise, you dine; at Ognisko, you live. Daquise remains an intimate, almost conspiratorial space, perfect for a quiet meal with a friend — or a co-conspirator. Ognisko, by contrast, is expansive and social. It is where weddings are toasted, debates are had, and where, on any given evening, one can encounter a mix of ambassadors, artists, academics, and at least one elderly Polish gentleman passionately discussing the betrayal at Yalta.

Of course, Polish cuisine in London is not limited to these two stalwarts. Mamuśka!, now located near Waterloo, brings a canteen-style, casual approach to Polish dining. It is where you go when you crave a hearty, no-nonsense meal — *bigos* that could sustain a Polish cavalryman, *schabowy* the size of a small country, and *pierogi* that require commitment. Mamuśka! embraces the boisterous, communal aspect of Polish eating; it is lively, affordable, and ideal for those who believe that food should be enjoyed with loud conversation and copious amounts of beer.

Bar Polski in Holborn, meanwhile, takes a different approach. It is the kind of place one might stumble into after work and then, several vodka shots later, stumble out of. Its focus on Poland's national spirit — offering a dizzying array of flavoured vodkas — makes it as much an education in Polish drinking culture as it is a dining experience. The food here is robust, designed to fortify those sampling the vodka selection, and while you may come for the *kielbasa*, you stay for the convivial atmosphere.

Then there are newer arrivals like Polka Kitchen and White Goose Bistro, adding their own interpretations to Polish cuisine. They bring a contemporary twist, offering refined takes on classic dishes, perfect for those who wish to experience Polish food in a setting that feels modern yet faithful to tradition. Another worthy mention is Autograf in North London, a hidden gem offering homestyle Polish food with generous portions and a no-frills, welcoming atmosphere. The dill-laden soups, expertly prepared *kotlet schabowy*, and delicate *pierogi* are reminiscent of a grandmother's kitchen, making it a favourite among both Poles and Londoners keen on an authentic experience.

One cannot overlook London's Polish bakeries, such as Koliba in Ealing or The Polish Bakery, known for its hearty rye bread and delicate pastries. These places serve as lifelines to the community, supplying London with *pączki* (Polish doughnuts), *makowiec* (poppy seed cake), and a variety of traditional sweets that can transport any Pole back to their childhood.

Another notable establishment is Łowiczanka, located within the Polish Social and Cultural Association (POSK) in Hammersmith. Situated on the first floor of this vibrant community centre, Łowiczanka offers a wide range of traditional Polish dishes in a friendly and unstuffy environment. Regular theme nights and dances, including live music on Saturday nights, add to its charm. The restaurant also caters to private parties, weddings, banquets, and social gatherings, making it a cornerstone for the Polish community in London. On 5 February 2025, King Charles III visited POSK. During his visit, His Majesty was served Polish delicacies prepared by Łowiczanka, showcasing the rich culinary heritage of Poland. The royal party and the guests enjoyed an array of traditional hot and cold dishes, further cementing Łowiczanka's place as a cultural and culinary landmark in London.

What unites all these establishments, beyond the food, is their role as cultural anchors. For decades, Polish restaurants in London have been more than places to eat; they have been places to gather, to remember, and to celebrate. They serve as a testament to the resilience of a community that has, at various points in history, found itself seeking refuge in Britain. Whether in the elegance of Ognisko, the historical gravitas of Daquise, the rowdy charm of Mamuśka!, or the vodka-infused revelry of Bar Polski, Polish cuisine in London offers something for everyone: a taste of home for those who miss it, and an invitation to discover for those who do not yet know it.

So, next time you find yourself in London, weary of overpriced small plates and avocado-based everything, step into a Polish restaurant. Order the *pierogi*, raise a glass of *żubrówka*, and toast to history, to friendship, and to the enduring appeal of good food served with warmth and wit.

Polish Footprints in London's Green Sanctuaries

London's parks hold secrets. Strolling beneath the ancient oaks of Hyde Park on a crisp morning, one might not immediately notice the subtle traces of Poland scattered among the greenery. Yet look closely and history reveals itself: a name on a memorial, the echo of foreign voices once raised at Speaker's Corner, or a lone wreath laid reverently beneath an eagle emblem. These green expanses — Hyde Park, Kensington Gardens, Hampstead Heath — are more than the lungs of London. They are living palimpsests of memory, where the story of Polish exile, resistance, and cultural continuity quietly entwines with Britain's own narrative of refuge and remembrance.

In Hyde Park, public life has long found a stage, from royal processions to impassioned protests. Here, in the relative tranquillity of the Serpentine's curve, one might still sense the resonance of a proposed yet unrealised gesture: a grand bronze Spitfire, soaring above the trees, to honour the Polish pilots who fought with unmatched bravery in the Battle of Britain. Though the monument never materialised, the very idea of it captured something indelible — the yearning to commemorate those who, in the words of one Polish Londoner, "spilt our blood" for Britain in its hour of need. Among them, the legendary 303 Squadron outpaced all others in courage and efficiency, their service written in the smoke-trails above Kent and Sussex, and in the quiet dignity of those who settled, after victory, far from home.

Hyde Park has heard Polish voices raised before. In December 1981, as martial law darkened Poland's skies, over 14,000 demonstrators gathered there in solidarity with Solidarność. Banners waved, prayers were murmured, and hopes were kindled in the winter air. It was one of the largest diaspora demonstrations London has seen — a powerful reminder that, far from Warsaw or Gdańsk, Hyde Park could still serve as a platform for freedom's cause. And yet, not all memories here are triumphant. In June 1946, London hosted its Victory Parade, a jubilant procession from Regent's Park through Oxford Street and down the Mall. Allied banners fluttered and marching bands played, but conspicuously absent were the Poles. Political expedience dictated that they be excluded from the official pageantry. Only a small token invitation was extended at the last moment — and was, in protest, declined. Thus the flag of a nation that had fought valiantly from the war's first day to its last did not appear among the victors. The silence of that omission echoed powerfully through the streets of central London, where applause rang for others. And though Hyde Park lay beyond the parade route, its own long avenues and open skies seemed to absorb something of the slight — a reminder that absence, too, can be a form of presence.

Just across from the park's southern edge, on Princes Gate, stands the Sikorski Institute and Museum, housed in a white stucco townhouse facing Kensington Road. Behind its elegant façade lies a trove of history: the archives of the Polish government-in-exile, painstakingly preserved — maps marked in haste, letters written in code, medals once pinned to the chests of forgotten heroes. It is a place of quiet reverence, a repository of a nation's will to endure, situated inconspicuously among embassies and institutions. A casual stroller on their way to the Serpentine might pass it without noticing, but within those walls beats a persistent echo of Poland's twentieth century, sheltered by London's architectural grace and the canopy of Hyde Park's ancient trees.

In nearby Kensington Gardens, the story of Polish exile takes a more contemplative turn. After the war, the tree-lined paths and tranquil ponds of this genteel quarter became a refuge for the displaced. One imagines émigré poets and professors, wrapped in overcoats too thin for London's damp, pacing the Round Pond in quiet conversation. For some, the gardens offered solace — a place to mourn a vanished homeland while teaching their children to ride bicycles or feed the ducks. The Polish Hearth Club, Ognisko Polskie, a short walk from the Royal Albert Hall, became the cultural heart of this community. In its modest garden, generals and writers exchanged news over steaming bowls of żurek, and decisions were made that would echo in Polish politics and letters for decades. The club's vine-covered courtyard became a sanctuary of its own — part embassy, part salon, wholly Polish.

Not far away, in Brompton Cemetery, Polish remembrance takes a more solemn form. Among its timeworn angels and ivy-covered headstones lie many exiles who never returned: airmen, officers, and civilian figures who lived out their days in quiet corners of London, their graves adorned with candles and chrysanthemums each November, as if London too celebrated All Souls' Day in Polish fashion. But one prominent name is absent. General Władysław Sikorski, wartime Prime Minister and commander-in-chief, was not laid to rest here but in Newark Cemetery, among fellow Polish airmen, before his reburial at Wawel Cathedral.

In London, his presence is honoured not by a tomb but by a monument: a dignified bronze bust mounted on a granite plinth, quietly standing at the corner of Portland Place and Weymouth Street, just beside the Polish Embassy and not far from Regent's Park. Unveiled at the turn of the millennium, it offers passers-by a moment of reflection — a leader in exile, remembered in the city that became his base and his burden.

The city's most solemn Polish monument, however, lies not in the royal parks but in a quieter precinct — Gunnersbury. There, in a modest cemetery, stands the Katyń Memorial: a black granite obelisk commemorating the 1940 massacre of over 20,000 Polish officers by the Soviet NKVD. For years, its creation was blocked, deemed too politically inconvenient. But in 1976, perseverance triumphed over diplomacy, and the monument was erected

— not in Kensington, as some had hoped, but here, amid trees and rose beds. Each spring, Polish families still gather around it, placing flowers and lighting votive lamps, ensuring that this grief, once denied, remains acknowledged. The trees bear silent witness; the grass, like memory, grows even over injustice.

Hampstead Heath offers a different sort of consolation. Untamed, unruly, and gloriously indifferent to the city's order, the Heath provided something akin to Poland's lost wilderness for artists and intellectuals in exile. Writers who once hiked the Tatra trails now trudged Parliament Hill, drawing strength from the wide skies and open views. In the years after the war, émigré painters captured the Heath's shifting light, finding in its contours a familiar melancholy. Today, on a summer's day, Polish families still picnic on its lawns, children tumbling down grassy slopes while elders sip tea and remember. It is not nostalgia so much as rootedness: a quiet sense that home can sometimes be conjured in leaf and sky.

To walk through London's parks, then, is to encounter not only natural beauty but also the ghosts and guardians of history. These green spaces, democratic and open, have long offered refuge and reflection to those far from their native soil. For the Polish community in Britain — soldiers, survivors, scholars, and shopkeepers — these parks became places where memory could be held, grief gently set down, and identity quietly sustained. A child feeding swans in Kensington may never know that a general once passed this way in exile. A jogger circling Hyde Park may be unaware that Polish voices once rose here in protest and pride. Yet these stories persist, quietly embedded in the grass, the paths, the trees.

London's parks are not just landscapes; they are sanctuaries of remembrance. In their meadows and margins lie the footnotes of Polish-British history, waiting to be read by those who walk with open eyes. Here, exile has found a place to rest. And here, under branches that know no borders, memory grows perennial.

A Diplomat's Sojourn: Navigating London's Gentlemen's Clubs

When I was appointed Poland's ambassador to the United Kingdom, an earnest yet somewhat provincial Polish politician approached me with a curious request: "When I visit London, you must invite me to one of these clubs." At the time, I was momentarily baffled, imagining he meant a lively jazz venue or perhaps an evening of revelry at an exclusive Mayfair establishment. It soon became clear, however, that he was referring to that most quintessentially British institution: the gentlemen's club.

As fate would have it, I never had to arrange an evening for that particular politician. Instead, my own initiation into this rarefied world came by invitation from our Foreign Minister, who welcomed me to White's, one of London's most storied gentlemen's clubs. Stepping through its doors was akin to entering a portal to another era — a realm where centuries-old conversations still seem to whisper in the oak-panelled rooms, and history manifests not merely as a backdrop but as a presence in itself. The club, established in 1693 as a chocolate house, has long been a sanctum of aristocrats, statesmen, and eccentrics, among them the Duke of Wellington, Winston Churchill, and even the occasional wayward prince.

London's clubland is a world apart, an ecosystem of institutions with distinct identities, each catering to a particular breed of member. I now count myself fortunate to belong to several: the Travellers Club, the Athenaeum, the Beefsteak Club, the National Liberal Club, and the Caledonian Club in Belgravia. Each has a history woven into the fabric of Britain's intellectual, artistic, and political life. The Travellers Club, founded in 1819, initially admitted only those who had ventured at least 500 miles beyond London — an extraordinary feat in an age when steam engines were still in their infancy. The Athenaeum, conceived in the 1820s, became a haven for scholars and creatives; its membership has included Charles Darwin, Dickens, and many of the great minds who shaped the modern world. The Beefsteak Club, dating to the eighteenth century, retains a more raffish charm, founded as it was by actors, artists, and literary wits, who no doubt consumed as much claret as they did beef.

Among these esteemed institutions, the Caledonian Club holds a special place in my affections. Founded in 1891, it stands as a bastion of Scottish culture and heritage in the heart of London, hosting Burns Night Suppers, St Andrew's Day celebrations, and gatherings that transport one momentarily to Edinburgh's New Town. Unlike many traditional gentlemen's clubs, the Caledonian embraced inclusivity earlier than most, admitting women as full members in 2010. Perhaps this progressive spirit derives from Scotland's own complex relationship with tradition — a reverence for history tempered by a readiness to adapt.

As a guest at White's, the Carlton Club, and the Army and Navy Club, I have witnessed firsthand the profound role these institutions play in fostering camaraderie, networking, and intellectual discourse. They offer refuge from the bustle of city life, providing a space where members may engage in lively debate over a port glass or sit in contemplative silence amid the leather-bound tomes of a club library. These establishments serve not only as retreats but as crucibles of influence, where ideas are exchanged over game pie and discussions begun in the smoking room may ripple outwards into the wider political world.

The absence of such institutions in Poland is, I must admit, a source of regret. We have no shortage of vibrant intellectual and cultural spaces — Warsaw's cafés and Kraków's literary salons have long nurtured creative minds — but we lack a tradition of private members' clubs devoted to particular professions or pursuits. Our history, fractured by partitions and upheavals, has rarely afforded us the luxury of continuity in such matters. And yet, one wonders whether Poland might benefit from fostering similar institutions, spaces where statesmen, writers, and scholars might exchange ideas in settings removed from the immediacy of politics.

Of course, London's gentlemen's clubs are not without their own internal tensions. In recent years, there has been much debate about their exclusivity, particularly regarding the admission of women. The Garrick Club, founded in 1831 as a refuge for actors and playwrights, only voted in May 2024 to admit female members for the first time — a decision that came after much agonising and more than a few resignations. It is a sign of the times, perhaps, that the most passionate opposition to reform often comes from those who would otherwise describe themselves as modern liberals. The change, inevitable as it was, represents not merely an adaptation to contemporary norms but an acknowledgment of the contributions women have long made to the worlds of theatre, literature, and public life.

Some lament these shifts, arguing that such institutions should remain frozen in time, guardians of a world that is vanishing. But even the most venerable clubs must evolve, lest they become mere museums, their relevance eroded by nostalgia. The best of them, I suspect, will adapt in ways that honour their traditions without ossifying them. That, after all, is the essence of British clubland: a paradoxical mix of rigidity and flexibility, where history is revered but where change, however grudgingly, is eventually accepted.

Perhaps Poland, too, could take inspiration from this. There is something undeniably valuable in the idea of a space where politics pauses, where conversation is cultivated for its own sake, and where the clink of a whisky glass signals not merely a toast, but the beginning of an idea that might, in its own way, shape history.

Afterword

The diplomat's work is often thought to begin and end at the conference table, but the more enduring business tends to happen elsewhere: over dinners that drift off-script, in side rooms where candour quietly replaces choreography, and in the long, unrecorded intervals between formal occasions. This book has followed those intervals — not to report on policy, but to reflect on the texture of relationship: not what is signed, but what is understood.

What began, for me, as a professional posting became something less official but more instructive: an exercise in attentiveness. It is one thing to know the history of a place; it is quite another to watch it surface, unbidden, in gestures, rituals, and unfinished conversations. Diplomacy, in that sense, is not a series of conclusions but a form of patient engagement. And this country — complex, self-aware, and fond of its own contradictions — rewarded engagement richly.

This is not a farewell, nor a summing-up. If anything, it is a pause. The ties between the nations at the heart of this book are not measured by proximity or protocol alone. They are composed of layered recognitions: shared silences in wartime cemeteries, footnotes in literary essays, bilingual menus in cafés whose staff speak both nostalgia and ambition. These things do not fit easily into communiqués, but they do endure.

Cultural diplomacy is sometimes treated as a softer substitute for the "real" work of statecraft. It is, in fact, the part most likely to last. History moves quickly now. Institutions change, borders flex, alliances shift tone. But poetry tends to outlive position papers, and the human instinct to understand across difference — however quietly it operates — has proven surprisingly resistant to obsolescence.

None of the essays in this collection claims to offer closure. That was never their purpose. They are fragments of an ongoing conversation: sometimes serious, sometimes amused, always provisional. They ask not to resolve, but to reflect. And perhaps, if they succeed, to remind us that the work of connection is not finished at the level of agreements — it begins, often, at the level of attention.

So the conversation continues. In other rooms, through other voices. And if these pages have managed to contribute even modestly to that dialogue, then they will have served their purpose.

ABOUT THE AUTHOR

Piotr Wilczek (born 1962) is a diplomat, scholar, and author. Before entering diplomatic service, he was a professor and academic administrator at the University of Silesia and the University of Warsaw. He has held visiting appointments at leading institutions including the University of Chicago, Rice University, the University of London, and the University of Oxford.

He served as Poland's Ambassador to the United States from 2016 to 2021, and as Ambassador to the United Kingdom from 2022 to 2026. In recognition of his contributions to education and international cooperation, he received an honorary doctorate from Cleveland State University in 2017.

The author of more than ten books and over one hundred scholarly articles on literature, history, and international affairs. His essays and commentary have appeared in *The Washington Post*, *The New York Times*, *The Daily Telegraph*, and *Monocle*.

ALSO BY PIOTR WILCZEK

Polonia Reformata: Essays on the Polish Reformation(s).
Vandenhoeck & Ruprecht: Göttingen, 2016. ISBN:
9783525552506.

*(Mis)translation and (Mis)interpretation: Polish Literature in the
Context of Cross-Cultural Communication.* Peter Lang: Frankfurt
am Main, 2005. ISBN: 9783631546284.

CHRONOS
BOOKS

HISTORY

Chronos Books is a historical nonfiction imprint. Chronos publishes real history for real people, bringing to life people, places, and events in an imaginative, easy-to-digest and accessible way — histories that pass on their stories to a generation of new readers.
If you have enjoyed this book, why not tell other readers by posting a review on your preferred book site.

Recent Bestsellers from Chronos Books Are:

Lady Katherine Knollys
The Unacknowledged Daughter of King Henry VIII
Sarah-Beth Watkins
A comprehensive account of Katherine Knollys's questionable paternity, her previously unexplored life in the Tudor court and her intriguing relationship with Elizabeth I.
Paperback: 978-1-78279-585-8 ebook: 978-1-78279-584-1

Cromwell was Framed
Ireland 1649
Tom Reilly
Revealed: The definitive research that proves the Irish nation owes Oliver Cromwell a huge posthumous apology for wrongly convicting him of civilian atrocities in 1649.
Paperback: 978-1-78279-516-2 ebook: 978-1-78279-515-5

Why The CIA Killed JFK and Malcolm X
The Secret Drug Trade in Laos
John Koerner
A new groundbreaking work presenting evidence that the CIA silenced JFK to protect its secret drug trade in Laos.
Paperback: 978-1-78279-701-2 ebook: 978-1-78279-700-5

The Disappearing Ninth Legion
A Popular History
Mark Olly
The Disappearing Ninth Legion examines hard evidence for the foundation, development, mysterious disappearance, or possible continuation of Rome's lost Legion.
Paperback: 978-1-84694-559-5 ebook: 978-1-84694-931-9

Beaten But Not Defeated
Siegfried Moos — A German anti-Nazi who settled in Britain
Merilyn Moos
Siegi Moos, an anti-Nazi and active member of the German
Communist Party, escaped Germany in 1933 and, exiled
in Britain, sought another route to the transformation of
capitalism.
Paperback: 978-1-78279-677-0 ebook: 978-1-78279-676-3

A Schoolboy's Wartime Letters
An evacuee's life in WWII — A Personal Memoir
Geoffrey Iley
A boy writes home during WWII, revealing his own
fascinating story, full of zest for life, information, and humour.
Paperback: 978-1-78279-504-9 ebook: 978-1-78279-503-2

The Life & Times of the Real Robyn Hoode
Mark Olly
A journey of discovery. The chronicles of the genuine
historical character, Robyn Hoode, and how he became
one of England's greatest legends.
Paperback: 978-1-78535-059-7 ebook: 978-1-78535-060-3